Major Themes in Contemporary Indian Fiction

Indian English fiction has witnessed a rapid growth in the last two decades. This phenomenon is the outcome of the broader realm of postcolonial literature. Indian fiction received a sudden spurt when Salman Rushdie, Arundhati Roy, Kiran Desai and Aravind Adiga received the coveted Booker Prize. Apart from these, other writers like Anita Desai, Manju Kapur, Jhumpa Lahiri, Shashi Deshpande and Shashi Tharoor introduced new themes and techniques, adding a rich variety to the corpus of Indian fiction. The present volume is devoted to some of the major themes dealt in the recent novels: mutliculturalism, history-fiction interface, women's issues, subaltern protest and the resurgent India.

Editor

Dr. Meeta Shukla is Associate Professor and Head, Department of English, D.A.V. College, Dehradun. Apart from doctoral degree on Carson McCullers from Kanpur University, she has obtained degree in Bachelor in Law (LLB) from HNB Garhwal University, and diploma in journalism from Vocational Institute of Christ Church College, Kanpur. She has presented scholarly papers at many conferences and also published various articles and books.

Major Themes in Contemporary Indian Fiction

Meeta Shukla

Prestige Books International
New Delhi

Published by
Prestige Books International
New Delhi 110 060
prestigebooks@gmail.com
Phone: 9818755529

Associate Office
50, Clapham Common Westside
London SW 49 A S, U.K.

Associate Office
P.O. Box 2250, Sydney 2001

ISBN: 978-93-82186-90-8

Printed in India

Contents

Major Trends in Indian English Fiction during Pre-Independence Era: An Overview

JAIDEEP CHAUHAN
S.D. College (Lahore) Ambala Cantt.

Indian novel in English has been regarded as a product of nineteenth century India. But the fact remains that the story-telling in India has a glorious past. K.R. Srinivasa Iyengar has rightly observed in his classic book *Two Cheers for the Commonwealth*:

> What can exist even in these days of sophistication the *Ramayana*, the *Mahabharata* or the *Iliad*? The banishment of drama on the very day fixed for coronation, the outrage of Draupadi in the Kaurava Court, The vengeful Bhima slacking his thirst in the blood of Dushasana, the killing of the sleeping warriors by Ashwathama, these are among the archetypes of human agony and superhuman endurance that take us back to the dawn of 'Civilization, the ultimate springs of the Jungian Collective conscious.' (137)

What is important to note is that there has been a remarkable tradition of story-telling in ancient India which clearly shows that the genre of novel writing/ story-writing did exist since the dawn of civilization in India. Let it be said at once here that the novel in the Western sense assumed distinct identity with the advent of the British in India. In other words, the conquest of India also became the conquest of narrative authority. The complex and the ambivalent role of English education, especially literary studies, determines the contours of Indian writing in English. Bernard Cohn in his essay "The Command of Language and the Language of Command" argues that the "conquest of India was a conquest of knowledge" (276) and as a result the British started a well-designed programme of appropriating Indian languages to serve as a critical component in their scheme of ruling India. The spread of English language in India and the interaction between the two races had its own inherent challenges. It goes without saying that literary conventions and discourses inherited from the colonizer were meticulously translated and appropriated to give a distinct shape to Indian writing in English. Cohn has a point when he suggests that

> The Indians who increasingly became drawn into the process of transformation of their own traditions and modes of thought were, however far from passive. In the long run the authoritative control which the British tried to exercise over new social and material technology was taken over by Indians and put to purposes which led to the ultimate erosion of British authority. (329)

The emergence of the novel in India, in fact, was partially guided by historical inevitability and complex cultural determinants which serve as a trigger to the creative imagination of the Indian writer.

Harish Trivedi in his *Colonial Transactions: English Literature and India* sees "the literary and cultural exchange between India and England as . . . one of the most vital and abiding aspects" of the Indian colonial experience (15). He observes, "not in the railways or the canals or the postal system or cricket or Christianity but rather in English and Indian literatures is to be found the deepest impress of the British Raj, the most permanent and authentic account of its process and proceedings"(15). The critic further argues that English literature in India has always coexisted in "a multi-lingual context" and hence this fact "affords another significant colonial perspective on it."

> It needs to be pointed out perhaps that some of these Indian writers are regarded as quite as significant in their own language as the

> English writers here discussed are in English. So Tagore rightfully occupies as much space here as any other writer Indian or English. (6)

It must be mentioned here that the earliest translations of English literature into Hindi date from the 1870s and among the earliest works to be translated were not only plays by Shakespeare—among which the early comedies were the favourites rather than say the four great tragedies (*Hamlet, Othello, Macbeth* and *King Lear*), which latter were in any case still to be definitively canonized by A.C. Bradley—but also somewhat surprisingly assorted works of the 18th century. Among the best known early translations into Hindi are the versions in the 1880s by Shridhar Pathak of several of Oliver Goldsmith's poems: *The Deserted Village* as *Ujar Gram, The Traveller* as *Shranta Pathik,* and *The Hermit* as *Ekantavasi Yogi*.

Pathak also translated Thomas Gray's "The Shepherd and The Philosopher," Longfellow's "Angelina" as well as his famous "Psalm of life" and James Thomson's "Rule Britannia." Among novels, Samuel Johnson's *Rasselas* was apparently a favourite and some of the earliest Hindi attempts at fiction of the Western kind, such as *Bhagyavati* (1879) by Pandit Shraddharam Phillauri and *Pariksha-Guru* (1884) by Lala Shrinivas Das (1851-87) were comparable moral and didactic tales. Such was the vogue for neo-classical, English literature that even a dodo of a work such as Addison's too correct and lifeless classical tragedy *Cato* was translated by Babu Tota Ram under the title *Kato Kritanta Natak* (1879).

The fact remains that the early novelists in India read British literature and translated some of the important literary works in Indian languages. Thus it is clear that the rise of the novel in India was not purely a literary phenomenon, it was a social phenomenon as much deeply associated with political and economic considerations prevalent in the 19th century India.

It is really important from the point of view of a study relating to the rise of novel in India that the years between 1818 and 1850 saw the emergence of prose as well as the appearance of journals and periodicals in most of the Indian languages. It was also a period of great social change and social thinkers like Raja Ram Mohan Roy exercised a profound civilizing influence on Indian psyche. Lord William Bentinck's Act of 1829 to end *Sati* paved the way for the emergence of individualist social order as against the traditional social and economic order. This was also the time when Calcutta was becoming the new economic Mecca drawing a vast migrant population looking for a new life and a new home. It is said that the modern Bengali was born from them and these Bengalis laid the foundation of prose writings in English in India.

The fact remains that the appearance of the novel in Bengali was neither purely accidental nor a result of the cross-cultural interaction between the natives and the colonizers. Two major works of fiction had been published in Bengal before the appearance of *Alaler Gharer Dulal*, the first Bengali novel in 1854. There were *A Journal of Forty Eight Hours of the Year 1845* by Kylash Chunder Dutt published in 1835 and *The Republic of Orissa: Annals from the Pages of 20th Century* by Sochee Chunder Dutt in 1845. It must be pointed out here at once that their claims as the first Indo-Anglian novels are open to controversy. That is why Pyari Chand Mitra's *Alaler Gharer Dulal* (1854) is still considered to be the first Bengali novel which is rather episodic in character. However, the first real Indian novels came into existence with the publication of Bankim Chandra's *Rajmohan's Wife* and Lal Behari Day's *Govinda Samanta*. It goes without saying that it was Bankim Chandra who established the novel as a major literary form in India. *Rajmohan's Wife* is the only English novel that he wrote and it appeared as serial in the *Indian Field* of 1854. It remains a fascinating text even after 150 years of its first publication. In India, the novel as a literary genre was in its infancy in 1864 and, while romance was widely acceptable as a narrative mode but there was no evident precedent as yet of mimetic rendering of domestic life in fiction or of weaving a plot out of contemporary social and familial situations. Meenakshi Mukherjee observes:

> There is also an attempt in *Rajmohan's Wife* to foreground the ways in which the home and the world are inextricably linked, a relationship which also happened to be of some concern to the classic realist novelists of nineteenth- century Europe, by locating the drama within the conjugal and domestic space in relation to the external arena of property, legality, crime and the colonial administration. (31)

The critic further adds that the other aspect of the novel that specially "intrigues us today is the language." When Bankimchandra, who was in the first graduating batch of the newly-founded Calcutta University, started writing *Rajmohan's Wife*, he must have known that the English-reading people of Bengal were not very widespread:

> Did he visualize clearly who was going to be his reader? The half-hearted attempts at textual explanations of cultural details suggest a vague awareness of readers who may be outsiders to the Bengali way of life—possibly the British administrators in India. . . . In *Rajmohan's Wife* Bankimchandra's attempts to negotiate the semantic and connotative hurdles that are involved in rendering an Indian (in this case Bengali) ethos in the English language, without any previous model whatsoever, forces us to think about the inter connectedness of culture and language, narrative voice and implied readership. . . (32)

Bankim's imaginative vigour and his sense of history added a new dimension to the art of novel writing in India. His contribution to the development of the Indian novel in English lay in the fact that he imaginatively adapted an alien form and language to a theme and sensibility which were essentially Indian. Humayun

Kabir discusses the contribution of Bankim to the art of novel writing:

> He sought human fulfilment through acceptance of the imperial and was in this respect influenced by Europe. Simultaneously, he sought to base the imperial on a total realization of knowledge, love and action, an impulse he derived from his Indian heritage. The European outlook is forward-looking where it is better to travel than to arrive for it, all experience is an arch . . . for India, novelty is not enough and must be based on deeper understanding or intuition of the whole. It was to Bankim's credit that he was able to effect a partial reconciliation between the contrary views. (39)

What Humayun Kabir seems to suggest is that Bankim Chandra was the first great Indian novelist who expressed the subtle nuances of his cultural mooring in English language in order to weave a figure in the carpet in the shape of a novel. The real question pertaining to the rise of novel in India lies in the fact that the early writers of fiction adopted some of the formal conventions of the Western novel in order to express their view embodies the authentic report of human experience pertaining to Indian culture and society.

Another milestone in the development of Indian novel in English is *Govinda Samanta.* Its appearance marked the birth of a new type of narrative prose-fiction in India. It is a novel written in a manner comparable to that of *Robinson Crusoe.* Its historical importance is exactly similar to that of Defoe and Richardson. One is reminded of what Ian Watt has written about Defoe and Richardson:

> Nevertheless there can be little doubt that the development of a narrative method capable of creating such an impression is the most conspicuous manifestation of that mutation of prose-fiction which we call the novel; the historical importance of Defoe and Richardson therefore primarily depends on the suddenness and completeness with which they brought into being what may be re-

> garded as the lowest common denominator of the novel genre as a whole, its formal realism. (34)

What Ian Watt says in the context of the rise of novel in England is also true from the point of view of the rise of novel in India. The rise of realism and individualism led to the new interpretation of historical and cultural values.

It would be in the fitness of things to consider the views of Meenakshi Mukherjee in *The Twice-Born Fiction* about the rise of the novel:

> If the social and literary conditions which gave rise to the novel in the Indian languages also brought forth the Indian novel in English, and if parallel trends can be observed in the Indo-Anglian novel as well as in the novels of the regional languages, then we must regard Indo-Anglian fiction as a branch of Indian fiction rather than of English fiction. Furthermore, if the Indo-Anglian novel is firmly rooted in the social and cultural ethos of India, then Indo-Anglian fiction has claims to be considered independently of the great tradition of the English novel. (33)

Social and cultural ethos of Indian society has played a very vital role in determining the contours of Indian novel in English. It would not be wrong to suggest that it is the crucial instrument whereby the novelist has expressed his moral sensibility. Social and cultural values of Indian society combined with literary perspective present in the age went into the making of the novel an art form. This also served as a deterrent to emotional artificiality. Indian novel, in its own way, reflects the process and highlights the ambivalent nature of cultural experience which constituted a challenge to the very foundations of the imperial rule.

The colonialist intervention during the early phase of the 19th century in a way revitalized the native languages and cultural values and these were deployed in the task of strengthening a sense of nationality. K.N. Panikkar writes of the curious position of the 19th century Indian intellectual whose internalization of the bourgeois-liberal colonialist ideology resulted in "the vision of a political future based on liberal and constitutional principles of the instrumentality of British rule" (21). Prominent 19th century intellectuals such as Keshub Chandra Sen, Lokhit Wadi and Raja Ram Mohan Roy at that time saw England as the liberator of Europe and thought that Indians could learn the art of democracy from their colonizers. However, at the same time they questioned and deplored the dumping of British manufactured goods in India and drain of wealth from India to England. It is true that the dominant British Raj made a consistent effort to impose its will on Indians but it failed to crush completely the socio-cultural ethos and novels written during the British Empire in one way or another were deeply rooted in the complex cultural atmosphere prevalent in India. The background of the rise of novel in India does point out that the colonial political framework had its own contradictions. As Rajeswari Sunder Rajan shows, Macaulay envisaged two important purposes of English education in India—"instrumental" and "integrative":

> The native elites too had no difficulty in accepting, and in fact in demanding, English education for the first purpose, as a means to security employment in the colonial bureaucracy or—more broadly—acquiring knowledge of Western sciences. The second they negotiated in various ways—through outright resistance to any trespass upon indigenous . . . or by more subtle forms of appropriation and a subversion of the values that were intended to mould them as subjects. (11-12)

Historically speaking, the first war of Indian independence, 1857 saw on the one hand the spread of the imperial attitude of the British, and the rise of the novel in India absorbing the eclectic tradition of learning and borrowing from the colonizers' literature and culture on the other. But the fact of the matter is that the appropriation absorption of foreign culture and language in no way subsided the interest in Indian culture and tradition. The Indians in fact in a way said a bold refusal to cultural dependency. The rise of the novel in India and the spread of British imperial mission in India went side by side. The classical justification of the empire was advanced by Lord Curzon and Lord Chamberlain but their justification was racist in nature. However, writers like John Seeley did not endorse the British imperial mission in India because of Indian inferiority. Rather he highlighted the merits of the ruled and wrote in no uncertain terms:

> We are not cleverer than the Hindu; our minds are not richer or larger than his. We cannot astonish him, as we astonish the barbarian, but putting before him ideas that he never dreamed of. He can match from his poetry our sublimest thoughts; ever our science perhaps has few conceptions that are altogether novel to him. (283)

It can be said that the ambivalent attitude towards British Empire and revival of interest in native languages, culture and tradition did play a crucial role in determining the nature of Indian fiction in English.

While there are a number of studies examining India/ Indian culture/ cultural values in relation to England and English literature, there is a distinct lack of profound critical studies in the Indian context with direct attention to England and the English. Harish Trivedi observes in response to the critique of Orientalism by the Western Academy:

> a parallel and salutary activity . . . to set beside it in the assimilative or subversive strategies through which we (Indian intellectuals) coped with their Orientalism. Furthermore, we could perhaps similarly parade some choice examples of our own occidentalism, which was a kind of comparable (mis-)knowledge with which we empowered ourselves to resist with the West. (20)

It must be pointed out here that in the whole history of British rule of India, few Englishmen could have paid an Indian writer more serious and sustained attention than Edward John Thompson (1886-1946) did Rabindranath Tagore (1861-1941). Thompson published two books on Tagore based on his study of Tagore's works in the original Bengali, a language he had learnt during his stay in India as a missionary teacher of English at Wesleyan College, Bankura (1910-23) and which he taught later as lecturer in Bengali at the University of Oxford (1923-33). He made it his own special concern to find ways of strengthening and promoting the cultural connection between India and England. He saw, according to Trivedi, "this bond as being of profounder and more enduring significance than the political relationship, of which he was in fact a prescient and deeply reflective elegist" (105-6).

The idea of knowledge/ mis-knowledge as an empowering strategy of resisting the West is in fact fascinating in the sense that the potential of subverting the relationship between the ruler and the ruled has immense possibilities because the British Empire failed to destabilize the foundations of Indian culture. The narrative form of the novel is fully equipped to do so and in the words of Barbara Harlow, is well suited to the task of subverting and appropriating Western traditions/ cultural values since it

> provides a more developed (compared to poetry) historical analysis of the circumstances of the economic, political and cultural domination and repression and through that analyses raises a systematic and concerted challenge to the imposed chronology of what Fredric Jameson has called 'master narratives,' ideological paradigms which contain within their plots a predetermined ending. The use by Third World resistance writers of the novel form as it has developed within the Western literary tradition both appropriates and challenges the historical and historicizing presuppositions, the narrative conclusions, implicated within the Western tradition and its development. (78)

The enterprise of representing culture/ cultural values in fiction allows for empowering the forces of occidentalism as described by Harish Trivedi.

To conclude we can say that the social, cultural and literary conditions have played an important role in the rise of the novel.

It would not be wrong to suggest that socio-cultural ethos of Indian society has played a very crucial role in determining the contours of Indian novel in English. In other words it can be said that it is the crucial instrument whereby the novelist has expressed his moral sensibility. Indian novel in its own peculiar way reflects the process and highlights the ambivalent nature of cultural experience which constituted a challenge to the very foundation of imperial rule.

Works Cited

Cohn, Bernard S. "The Command of Language and the Language of Command." *Subaltern Studies* IV.

Harlow, Barbara. *Resistance Literature.* London: Methuen, 1987.

Iyengar, K.R. Srinivasa. *Two Cheers for the Commonwealth.* Bombay: Asia, 1970.

Mukherjee, Meenakshi. *The Twice-Born Fiction: Themes and Techniques of the Indian Novel in English.* Delhi: Pencraft International, 2010.

Panikkar, K.N. *Culture, Ideology, Hegemony: Intellectuals and Social Consciousness in Colonial India*. New Delhi: Tulika, 1995.

Rajan, Rajeswari Sunder. *The Lie of the Land.* Oxford UP, 1997.

Seeley, J.R. *The Expansion of England*. London: Macmillan, 1920.

Trivedi, Harish. *Colonial Transactions*. New York: Manchester, 1993.

Watt, Ian. *The Rise of Novel*. London: Pimlico, 2000.

Feminism in the Fiction of Nayantara Sahgal

MEETA SHUKLA
D.A.V. (P.G.) College, Dehradun

Some of the most prolific Indian women writers who have made a notable contribution in feminist writing are Shashi Deshpande, Anita Desai, Bharati Mukherjee, Kamala Markandaya, Shobha De, Ruth Prawer Jhabvala and Nayantara Sahgal. Of these, Nayantara Sahgal's writings are unique since they are largely based on the first hand experience of urban upper-middle class, of which she was a part. As a member of the Nehru-Gandhi family, the second of the three daughters born to Jawaharlal Nehru's sister, Vijaya Lakshmi Pandit, she had a close understanding of the elite classes. Belonging to such a famous and powerful political family, her writings are distinctly political and contemporary. Her hallmark is widely believed to be her ability to interweave various pressing issues afflicting women into this very socio-political setting.

Winner of the coveted Sahitya Akademi award and Sinclair Prize, Nayantara Sahgal was one of the tallest literary figures in postcolonial India. Like most of the women authors of the period then and arguably even now, her writings are considered as focussed on the plight of women and the crying need for their emancipation. True to form, Sahgal's protagonists in her many novels, however, are not the weak and ordinary women-folk; they are invariably the well heeled, or political or working class modern upper circle women. However, they too have been shown to suffer discrimination, erosion of their identity and suppression at all stages.

She was one of the first female Indian writers in English to receive wide recognition. Selected collection of letters exchanged between Sahgal and her second husband Rai was published in the book *Relationship*. When it was published in 1994, it was received with both shock and appreciation. The letters highlight one woman's endeavour to remain true to herself, her writing, her ideals and relationships, both outside and within marriage. Her literary bag includes eight novels, two autobiographies and some non-fictional works. Several articles and short stories of her have been published in leading newspapers and magazines.

Interestingly, there are two contrarian view-points on Nayantara Sahgal as a feminist writer. Feminism may be simply defined as 'The advocacy of women's rights on the grounds of equality of sexes.'[1] Feminist writers, in their works, depict marriage as an emotionally stifling and tyrannical institution for women. Their characters are victims of gender-oppression, where marriage for a man means enlargement of his existence. He enjoys both the worlds: of home and of career. It permits him progression and self-advancement. In marriage, oneness, companionship and mutuality are stressed, and it is assumed that the interests of the husband and wife are one. Despite these idealized concepts of marriage, woman in reality is shown as essentially a subservient partner in marriage. Marriage often does not mean companionship or equality for her; rather it is a trap which negates her rights to individuality and independence. The writers depict the institution of marriage as one that consistently denigrates the status of women. She is subjugated, marginalized and sidelined and usually her position is no better than those subjected to racial prejudices.

In many ways, Sahgal's writings are no different. She articulates with sensitivity the problems and sufferings of women in marriage, who feel entrapped, oppressed and doomed to the care of husband and home. She beautifully showcases their reaction to it in their novels. Some of the women accept their fate unhesitatingly, but most of them yearn for freedom, and gradually reject the stereotype by going in for separation or for divorce to live a meaningful life. A fair attempt at voicing female concerns is visible in Nayantara Sahgal's writings. Most of her protagonists refuse to accept the schism in sexes. They do not want to define themselves in relation to men and hence seek identity and independence in their own way. When they realize that they are being used, they turn insubordinate, being non-submissive and non-conforming, asserting their individuality.

This viewpoint is backed up in *The Day in Shadow* is critiqued. Som, a business magnate in the novel, draws pleasure in showing off his wife as his property. He treats his wife Simrit as a valued object for his personal pleasure. He is happy with the thought that his job is over as a husband by bedecking his wife with jewellery and expensive clothing. Simrit, however, finds the materialistic world of Som worthless. She craves for a meaning beyond the world of self-advancement, a world whose texture was kindly.[2] She feels she has lived half of her life as a submissive and conforming person; henceforth, she is going to be a free being. Som agrees to divorce his wife for monetary benefit. He imposes cruel divorce terms on his wife in order to take revenge on her. Simrit continues to suffer till she finds a messiah in Raj who protects her and later marries her. Simrit does not leave Som for Raj's sake; she only shares his friendliness and tenderness, though later both get married. With Raj she has a more involved relationship. Raj not only shakes her benumbed mind but makes her live as a bold and assertive woman. However, as the novel goes on to subtly reveal, ironically the patriarchal attitudes are shown as embedded in Raj too. And this is where Nayantara Sahgal comes under some scrutiny for her incomplete and mixed up crusade for feminist goals. Notwithstanding this, this is one conventional interpretative approach to Sahgal's writings.

Herein lies the counter viewpoint mentioned earlier in this paper. The issue of this mixed up crusade, related to patriarchy and imperialism can be well understood by a review of her *Rich like Us*. This novel has been overwhelmingly praised by critics as an excellent political fiction, winning her the Sahitya Akademi Award and the Sinclair Prize.[3]

Born into modern India's premier political family, the Nehrus, Nayantara was brought up in a family in which female children did not feel the pressure of their gender. She proves to be very much a product of such upbringing and her sense of nationalism is significantly coloured by it. Sahgal relegates the issue of feminity to the national issues in her works. Ironically, but not surprisingly, her allegiance to nationalism is coloured by her Western upbringing and education, not helped in the least by her personal location in an international setting, rather than a local literary playing field, resulting in multiple contradictions in her novel. This international setting made her outlook Eurocentric and deviated her significantly from a 'true' depiction of what an oppressed woman in a mass Indian setting ought to be. Nayantara Sahgal ends up creating in *Rich like Us* a contradictory discourse; removed from the oppressed Indian woman.

In this novel, she focuses on two female protagonists, Sonali and Rose, and makes an involved bid to champion the cause of women. But as one takes a closer look at how this novel pans out, and when one compares it with other non-western Indian women writers, Nayantara Sahgal does not come up as someone who has done full justice to her characters in their fight for true female emancipation. It would not be incorrect to say that in her novels there is only a limited commitment to what one would have wanted to see from an ardent advocate of feminism.

In an interview, Nayantara Sahgal said, "It is very difficult to separate politics from real life in India, as the reality of life is so political here where women are roasted alive on their husband's funeral pyres and are burnt to death for dowry."[4] The conclusion this paper drives from her readings is that the issues of suttee and dowry harassment have been exploited by her not for voicing feminist concerns, but merely as a take-off point, or a platform for her nationalist outpourings.

She is also known to have said in a 1997 interview, "I have never written from any specific ideological viewpoint. If I have, I have a nationalistic viewpoint."[5] Therefore it would not be incorrect to say that it is this nationalistic hankering that is responsible for Sahgal's misplaced coverage of nationalist discourse with the discourse on women. This led to a relative muting of the concerns and problems of women in her novels. Somewhere she appears to have got a bit muddled up in this process, and at the altar of nationalism, the feminine issues have taken a backseat.

Since she was much in the influence of her well connected influential family members, it would also be apt to take a look at what they held forth on the subject. It may be noted that Mrs. Gandhi herself never agreed that she was a feminist or a specific champion of female rights. Unencumbered by her gender, she had stated, "I always felt that I could do anything I wanted."[6] In fact she is known to have stated that of all the female characters in our ancient mythology, Sita stands out as a shining beacon of an exemplary Indian woman with her self-sacrificing and 'loyalty to husband' credentials. Thus there is significant ambivalence in Nayantara Sahgal's writings when it comes to issues of feminism. She duly exhibits the effect of her political upbringing and feels that nationalism is one unifying force that circumvents all social and religious barriers, including gender. As a feminist, if at all, Nayantara Sahgal would have been expected to not undermine the issue of gender at the altar of nationalism.

While Sonali is vehemently critical of the reach and power exerted by the men folk in a marriage, she still looks up to men only, ranging from her father to other acquaintances, to guide her, and for her emancipation and protection. She says, "I only blame Papa that . . . he gave me no advice. He could have said, You should resign." This happens at a stage in the novel when Sonali is as much as thirty eight years old and has had a fifteen year experience in a high position in the Indian Civil Service. In keeping with the male superiority centric refrain in Indian history, she believes that the most admired national heroes are all men—the Gandhis, Nehrus etc. So Sonali, the main protagonist in the novel, cannot be viewed as a committed and true blood feminist voice.

Additionally, not only is Sonali's role as an ardent feminist questionable, but Sahgal's treatment of the other protagonist in the novel, Rose as the suffering Hindu wife too is paradoxical. Rose is shown as reconciling herself to her husband's continued philandering, without making a fight out of it. Here again, Nayantara's feminist leanings become weak, affected by her elitist upbringing. The nationalist narrative by Sahgal ends up colouring and adversely affecting her feminist coverage. By giving primacy to a nationalist political narrative in *Rich like Us*, Sahgal unwittingly, but decisively nonetheless, becomes a complicit partner in tolerance of oppression of Indian women. Stuart Hood remarked that Sahgal is "not an Indian writer" but an English writer working in a tradition that is hers by birth, education and class.[8]

In conclusion, Sahgal's protagonists in her many novels, invariably the political and working class modern upper circle women, suffer discrimination, erosion of their identity and suppression at all stages. There is no denying that Sahgal strongly condemns the attitudes which reduce woman to an object.

However, it is to be noted that Sahgal is not a staunch feminist and subscribes only to the idea of it, and not to every aspect of it. The author believes she ended up avoiding going into the depths of a woman's mind, and left her treatment of feminist issue half-baked. She may have unwittingly done so in two ways.

One, as penned in novels like *The Day in Shadow*, she remained focussed principally on the physical aspects of the need for a new social order, divorce, and securing release though extra-matrimonial relationships. The other was as evidenced in *Rich like Us*, where she may have been complicit in using issues afflicting the women as a bulwark for her nationalistic cravings and writings thereof. Thus, while she may have dealt with the disintegration of relationships and marriages in a typical Indian setting beautifully, her writings can be deemed as more upper crust feminism in flavour, and delving relatively superficially on the root causes and impediments in the way of women empowerment.

NOTES

1. https://en.oxforddictionaries.com/definition/feminism.
2. Nayantara Sahgal, *The Day in Shadow*, Calcutta: Penguin, 1971.
3. https://en.wikipedia.org/wiki/Nayantara_Sahgal.
4. V. Mohini, "Writer at Work: Nayantara Sahgal," *The Literary Criterion*, 25.1 (1990), p. 62.
5. *Cognitive Discourses International Multidisciplinary Journal*. Vol. 1: 3, November 2013, http:cdimj.naspublishers.com.
6. H.S. Mann, *Elliptic Feminism and Nationalism in Nayantara Sahgal's Rich like Us*, Loyola University, Chicago.
7. Ibid.
8. Stuart Hood, "Shadows," *The Times Literary Supplement*, June 26, 1969, p. 6.

Language and Postcolonialism: Anita Desai's *In Custody*

MEGHANA J.R.
Directorate of Distance Ed., Kuvempu University

Anita Desai, born on 24 June 1937, is an Indian novelist. She has been shortlisted for the Booker Prize three times; she received Sahitya Akademi Award in 1978 for her novel *Fire on the Mountain*. She won the British Guardian Prize for *The Village by the Sea*. In 1993, her novel *In Custody* was adopted by Merchant Ivory Productions into an English film by the same name, directed by Ismail Merchant, with a screenplay by Shahrukh Hussain. It won the 1994 President of India gold Medal for Best film and stars Shashi Kapoor, Shabana Azmi and Om Puri.

The term postcolonialism is certainly one of the most actively debated terms in the contemporary literary criticism and socio-political studies. Like many romantic and post-romantic workers Anita Desai's *In Custody* derives its structure from a series of climatic perfect moments and epiphanies which provide solace and meaning for Deven's life. The complexities to undermine the language struggle are political, economic and social; here is the failure of tradition and modernity going hand in hand. Urdu poetry is like any other divine poetry based on love but after Indian freedom the practical situation does not help it.

To show the reciprocation of multiculturalism to post-Independence literature, Desai describes the meetings in the house of Nur in the evenings. Nur's house is supposed to have some gathering where the visitors are divided into camps like "Persian camp, Hindustani camp, Pakistan camp." Deven's meetings with Murad always suggest latter's desire to earn money and be a superior person. However disillusionment is visible in Anita Desai's literary rebukes to the intellectual as well.

Like Fernando's *Three Women*, Anita Desai's *In Custody* criticizes traditional society; her novel focuses on a pathetic, trapped male character whose wife despises his inability to succeed financially. A terrified, insignificant person, Deven moves from mediocrity as a college lecturer to professional and financial ruin as he incurs increasing monetary debts, which he finally decides to endure rather than committing suicide. His wife gives him little support; in fact, the women in the book seem rather nasty, especially the enraged young wife of Deven's hero, the poet Nur. As the story progresses, we see the male characters trapped in a world that offers no possibility for success, they feel frustrated with a sexist society that reduces them to clinging to those who cannot provide them with what they want.

Desai shocks us near the end of her novel when she presents Nur's young wife's point of view in a letter to Deven in which she claims that Nur married her because of her gifts and abilities; she challenges him to read her enclosed poems. Deven's timidity prevents her defiant letter from gaining her acceptance in the world of Urdu poetry; he tears up her poems. But her angry statements make the reader re-evaluate what they had previously seen through the eyes of male characters only. By making women's frustration understandable, Desai subverts her book's primary unsympathetic portrayals of women which turn out to have been Deven's, and not author's, perceptions.

The language of Anita Desai is poetic and engaging and it adds to the charm of this novel. My Hindu blood boiled with rage in initial few pages when I saw Nur and his friends calling Hindiwallah's vegetarian monsters while placing Urdu on a high pedestal. But it became clear that the joke is indeed on them as those who rely on the purity of a language actually defile it with their gluttony and immortality. A language can't survive in hands of such puppets of lust and debauchery. But Deven took a lot of time to understand this subtlety and thus loses not just his money, time and energy but also the support of his own family and friends. He misses the reader's sympathy for his stupidity and his infallible belief in frail debauched, gluttonous man, allowing himself to be taken advantage of by barbaric people who are milking Urdu ceaselessly for their own petty benefits.

Desai centres *In Custody* around Deven whose essentialist concept of woman leads to his failure. For one brief moment, Desai hints at the unrealized potential in Deven's relation to women when she describes him listening to Nur's wife recite poetry: "The elegance and floridity of her Urdu entered Deven's ears like a flourish of trumpets and beat at his temples while he read." The essential, unsuspected spirit of the woman appeared to step free of its covering, all the tinsel and gauze and tawdriness, and reveal a face from which the paint and powder had been washed and which wore an expression that made Deven halt and stumble before he could read on. This man has devoted himself to the propagation and proper documentation of Urdu poetry, yet he does not have the courage to read the poetry of a woman only because she is a woman. The most potent embodiment of this idea is found within this woman's letter, in which she asks Deven: "Are you not guilty of assuming that because you are a male, you have a right to brains, talent, reputation and achievement, while I, because I was born female, am condemned to find what satisfaction I can in being maligned, mocked, ignored and neglected? Is it not you who has made me play the role of the loose woman in gaudy garments by refusing to take my work seriously and giving me just that much regard that you would extend to even a failure in the arts as long as the artist was male? In this unfair world that you have created what else could I have been but what I am?"

This recognition is not a general one. For example, instead of reacting to the disturbingly tragic and frustrating conclusion, culminating in Deven's dismissal of the women from his life, Richard Cronin, who finds that the novel had an optimistic ending, sees Desai as identifying with Deven! Deven, the quiet man, will never be able to extricate himself from Nur and his noisy household. It is a predicament that Anita Desai understands. In seeking to be the custodian of India she has herself been taken into custody, has placed her quiet, fastidious talent at the service of a noisy, melodramatic land. It is a painful burden. So Deven feels, and one senses that Anita Desai sometimes finds it so. But *In Custody* ends not with a gesture of weariness but with Deven striding robustly forwards, confident that the burden he has condemned himself to carry is also his highest honour.

Cronin writes in his introduction that the goal of his attempt to "imagine India" is to locate his own sense of power and authority. Expounding upon novels written by Indian authors would serve, for Cronin, as "the ground of my authority--it would have become the perspective that enabled me to summon one after another a dozen different Indias while remaining myself aloof from them." In contrast to Cronin's interpretation of Desai's writing, R.S. Pathak recognizes Desai's intentions as seeking to highlight the status of women in society. Pathak thus addresses the character of Sarla, Deven's wife, who is notably absent in Cronin's critique. Sarla's miserable, routine life, full of labour, "the shabbiness of her limp, worn clothes, or her hunched, twisted posture, her untidy hair or sullen expression, were all integral parts of her humiliation." Anita Desai's novels are, in a way, an advocacy for the legitimate rights and freedom of such unfortunate women.

In Custody attacks the social structure that dictates the roles and interactions of its characters. Pathak discerns a potently political commentary in Desai's work that counters the optimism identified by Cronin: Anita Desai has conveyed her women characters' fundamental dependence on men through her lexicon and tropes of mastery, command and domination. Her women sometimes do attempt to assert their independence and self-sufficiency, but their quest for identity is thwarted at significant junctures. No woman in Anita Desai's novels has been fortunate enough to free herself from the shackles of femininity.

In Custody is slightly different from Anita Desai's previous novels. This novel is about postcolonialism in India after the British Rule. First, the story is not about a woman. In fact, the protagonist, villain and all main characters are men. So, essentially, she leaves her safe area of femininity to delve into the adrenaline packed, loud male world. The dominating Ishiana Begum and Deven's wife are not given centre-stage and are there to simply aggravate Deven's problems, acting as foil to the main antagonists. In short, Deven shines as the real anti-hero of this novel. Further, unlike her previous novels like *Fasting Feasting*, the protagonist is not suffering from any serious tragedy. He is simply a naive man, without any definite goals in life. He is made to look like a fool by almost everybody. His good nature aids in his fall and gravely pushes him into a dark recess. And despite his continual dismal condition, he is denied readers' sympathy as the author presents him in a lighter vein, declaring him to be aloof and ill-fit to survive in this world.

Many modern gadgets like Tape recorder are used to record the voice of Nur. At the end, Deven is hopeful that he will be able to record Nur's poetry and get some relief from his misery.

Depression in Kamala Das' *My Story*

V. SRILATHA
Stanley College of Engg. & Tech. for Women, Hyderabad

Kamala Das, the eminent writer in English and Malayalam languages is the author of many novels, collections of short stories and poetry. She is the recipient of awards like Sahitya Akademi Award, Vayalar Award and Kerala Sahitya Akademi Award. *My Story*, the autobiography became sensational with the articulation of the incidents of her life. The book *My Story* was published originally in Malayalam entitled *Ente Katha*. Later the book was not just translated, but revised and rewritten in English.

Kamala Das does not get love and affection from her parents. She feels neglected by them as she is a dark girl with ordinary features. She reveals that her father has little time to show his affection on his children while her mother, a writer, is almost engaged in writing. Kamala and her brother face discrimination at their European school. She says that her white classmates at their school used to make fun of her brother as he is plump and dark, though he is clever in the class. She even reveals that the brown children are discreetly hidden away in the lavatories with the school ayas for company, whenever there are distinguished visitors in the school.

Kamala starts composing poems during her school days. Once her poem is recited by a cute Scot girl called Shirley and Kamala feels marginalized when the principal has readily attributes the authorship to the girl in front of the visitors. Even she has written poems of dolls that have lost their heads and have to remain headless for clarity.

These dolls symbolize the fear of the loss of identity and selfhood of the author. Kamala feels frustrated with the racial discrimination at the European school and lack of affection from parents. "I wondered why I was born to Indian parents instead of to a white couple who may have been proud of my verses." (9)

Her father is indifferent towards her. He joins her into boarding school and later does not bother her. He does not care for her even on her birthdays. Once Kamala's grandmother asks Kamala's uncle to get some cloth for the frock for Kamala on her birthday. Her grandmother does not know the latest trend and she could not afford to buy her silks. When Kamala accompanies her uncle to city bazaar, he asks the salesman to show some inexpensive cloth. As there is nothing cheaper, her uncle shouts at him, Kamala feels humiliated. "I wanted like Sita to disappear into the bowels of the earth." (40)

When Kamala shows her dress to her room-mates at her boarding school, they are disappointed, but Kamala convinces them that she is going to get her birthday frock from Calcutta by her father. Even the Calcutta frock does not reach in time. Kamala's room-mate Sarada says that she wants to buy a nice dress for her cousin, Satyavati and asks Kamala to select one of her choice. Kamala is amazed to see the lovely fabrics and picks one for Satyavati. Surprisingly, she gives the same dress to Kamala on her birthday. Kamala weeps hiding her face in Sarada's hair.

Kamala wants to lead a rich, happy and comfortable life. Once she prays God to make her rich enough to live in an old mansion. She wants to marry a rich man, 'a zamindar' and live in the city of Calcutta. She wishes to be a snob, but feels disappointed that her life has been planned and cannot dream to alter anything. Her life has been planned by her parents and relatives. She realizes that she has to be the victim of a young man's carnal desire and perhaps get a few children.

She imagines that she is going to be a middle-class housewife walking along the vegetable shop carrying a string bag and wearing faded chappals on her feet. She visualizes that her children would be asking for expensive toys which they cannot afford.

The trauma and oppressive sense of loneliness and alienation of her childhood continues even in her adulthood. Kamala's mother goes to Malabar after recovering from illness, along with Kamala's younger brother and sister for taking rest. Even her elder brother goes to Madras to pursue his medicine. She is left alone with her father in Calcutta. It is a period of intense loneliness for her. She finds no one to bother her. She feels as an intruder in her own house other than her room. She resolves to raise herself from the desolation of her life and escape into another life and into another country.

Kamala cannot express her feelings to her father that she neither likes the person nor is ready to marry then. Out of respect towards her father she agrees to marry him. She knows that neither her parents nor her grandmother has patience to bear the burden of the unmarried girl. Moreover nobody asks her whether Kamala likes to marry him or not. It is taken for granted. Her grandmother comes and tells her that her parents are willing to marry her to Das. "Das is a very good young man and entirely without vices. Your parents and his mother feel that you two should get married soon." (77) She feels desolated and lonely. She wishes to marry a person who maintains more tranquil relationship with her; understands her and supports her but in vain. "I felt lost and unhappy. I could not tell my father that I had hoped for a more tranquil relationship with a hand on my hair and a voice in my ear, telling me that everything was going to be all right for me." (80) Kamala feels very much disappointed with her arranged marriage and does not know whom to take advice from. Marriage does not give any kind of solace and happiness, rather it is "unsatisfying and unfulfilling" (Pathak). She wants to escape but in vain.

On her wedding night she requests her husband to pray to Lord Krishna, but he gives deaf ears and seduces her. The next morning she could not move her limbs and feels tears in her eyes. She is deeply in love with her husband and is ready to bear any torture, but her immature body does not support love-making.

Kamala loves Lord Krishna. When she expects a baby, she tells her grandmother that her son is moving in her womb. When her grandmother asks how she could tell that the child is a son, she tells her grandmother confidently that she is going to get a boy who resembles Lord Krishna. She dreams about Krishna, "Through the smoke of the incense I saw the beauteous smile of my Krishna. 'Always, always, I shall love you,' I told him, not speaking aloud but willing him to hear me, 'only you will be my husband, only your horoscope will match with mine.'" (87)

When Kamala delivers a baby, she feels elated and invites her husband to Malabar. He visits her, but grows disgusted when the child disturbs several times during night times to take his feed. Kamala observes that her husband has spent most of his time with his cousins and sister-in-law. He never bothers to converse with her. She yearns for love and feels that "All the Parijata that I wove in my curly hair was wasted." (89)

Kamala expects her husband to treat her as a wife and honour her. She finds that the only topic of conversation that delights her husband is sex. She realizes that her husband married her for social status and the possibility of financial gain and feels disappointed. Her struggle to get the expected love becomes futile. "I wanted to be given an identity that was lovable." (90) Her mother-in-law grows visibly upset and sulks for every domestic inconvenience. She says disgruntled things and Kamala's husband becomes annoyed and directs his anger on Kamala and the baby. Kamala says even the servants could not get on with her mother-in-law. Kamala is hardly fifteen. She likes to play hop-scotch, but her mother-in-law complains that she is away from her child and domestic responsibilities for most of the time. Even Kamala's husband stops her from going up onto the terrace for the rehearsals in the evening. "You must remember you are a wife and mother." (93)

Looking at the situations and listening to the conditions and restrictions, Kamala's ego is hurt. She feels: "I am the beloved and the Betrayed. I have no joys which are not yours, no Aches which are not yours. I too call myself I" (Tarun 2). One day as she could not bear it any longer, sends a cook to a chemist shop for a dozen tablets of barbiturates to commit suicide but, the cook returns empty-handed. Kamala tries to settle down by making herself busy with the household work, but she feels that her spirit protested and cried to get out of this trap and escape.

Kamala feels alienated as her husband is indifferent towards her. "My husband was nearly all the time away touring in the outer districts. Even while he was with me, we had no mental contact with each other. If at all I began to talk of my unhappiness, he changed the topic immediately and walked away" (147).

Kamala's husband is apathetic. He does not find time to his family. He does not bother to receive Kamala from airport even during late hours, besides that he comments that she is late. Kamala is disheartened. When she asks for the reason for not receiving her at the airport, he merely says that he is tired and sleepy and will talk the next day. Kamala's husband "was crude, insensitive and incapable of basic human decency" (shodhganga). He cannot bear the inconvenience and shouts at his crying son at midnight. Being busy with his official report he locks up the baby once in the kitchen and leaves him to lie on the cold kitchen floor. Kamala feels miserable but she does not indulge in argument.

During her husband's stay in Orissa, her son eats castor seeds and becomes sick. She feels that she is "like a house with all the lights put out." At that time her husband comes along with his old friend and to celebrate her birthday they send Kamala out of their bedroom and lock themselves in. She feels disgusted and wants to die. "I wanted for a moment to fling myself down, to spatter the blanched brilliance of the moonlight with blood stains. . . . I felt then that I was dancing on the desolate pinnacle of the world. The dance of the last human being." (99)

She understands that there is goodwill between the two families and does not admit to anyone that her marriage has flopped. She believes that a broken marriage is distasteful and horrifying. She says that if she goes by conscience and leaves her husband it would be impossible to find another to marry her, besides this, she feels that she is not so beautiful and her two-year-old son may become an "encumbrance."

During her pregnancy, she becomes addicted to drinking "Draksharishta" an ayurvedic preparation made from grapes and molasses. She gets relaxation with the drink which intoxicates her and removes all bitterness experienced in her life and makes her feel happy and comfortable. After her second delivery, her uneasiness increases and she wishes to escape from her home and walk till the end of the world, but her ignorance makes her walk and reach the sea shore of Danda, but the turbulence of the sea only aggravates her restlessness. This restlessness and depression in Kamala Das is mainly because of her attitude towards men. "Kamala Das has been fiercely rebellious against the male section of the society for the emotional and psychological torture inflicted on her by husband in marital life and by lovers in extramarital relationship." (Prasanna Sree) Kamala does not want to die though she is admitted in hospital for several reasons. Once she feels that she is going to die, but Mrs. Karunakaran, a doctor, saves her. She is delighted and strokes her hair and kisses her.

Kamala acts as a Judge at Trivandrum and grows many enemies. They even have tried to kill her: "they buried an urn somewhere in my yard, hoping to kill me with the rites of sorcery." She even dreams that death has come to her as a woodpecker and has begun to peck her bones.

She suffers from Leukemia. Even after moving into the Bombay hospital, she imagines a man and addresses him as Krishna and feels his love in her dreams. She becomes sick frequently and her loneliness makes her visualize her death "I was looking into the depths of my loneliness. Then I felt that I was applying paint on the lips of a corpse" (180).

She goes into depression with her loneliness, her financial crisis, her yearning for love which she could not get; and the strange situations which she encounters. She compares her life with the trees and realizes that everything has to perish in life. She tunes her mind finally and becomes content. "Perhaps I shall die soon. . . . And yet the world shall go on. . . . My descendants shall populate this earth. It is enough for me. It is more than enough." (214)

Works Cited

Das, Kamala. *My Story*. New Delhi: Harper Collins, 2009.

"Kamala Das's *My Story*: An Evaluation" (shodhganga.inflibnet.ac.in).

Pathak, Rajdeep. *Indian Writing in English and Kamala Das* (www.bologi.com).

Prasanna Sree S *Alien among Us; Reflections of Women Writers on Women*. New Delhi: Sarup, 2008.

Rawal, Tarun D. "Quest for Female Identity in Kamala Das." *Galaxy: International Multidisciplinary Research Journal*, II: V, 2013.

A Study on the "Feministic Ideologies" in Shobha De's *Socialite Evenings* and *Sisters*

RANGANATH BILLAR B.
Government First Grade College, Manvi, Dt. Raichur

The term feminism is derived from the Latin word 'Femina' which means women. It is associated with female agitational movement. Feminism means struggle and rebellion to attain social, racial, economic, political, and spiritual equality with men. Alexander Dumas the French playwright coined the term 'Feminism.' In the year 1928 Virginia Woolf delivered a modest lecture "A Room of One's Own" which had foreseen results and interpretations even today, regarding the status and role of women. Simon de Beauvoir's *The Second Sex* deals with feminist ideologies and concentrates on the facts and myths about woman. Indian women writing in English received a great impetus from the feministic movements which sprouted from the west. Recently feminist movement is also associating with gay, lesbian, and other libertarian agitations.

The purpose of this paper is to focus on the two novels of Shobha De, *Socialite Evenings* and *Sisters*, and to analyze the text to identify and co-relate themes of feminism associated ideologies with her characters, and how her characters ensnared in the tumultuous and tyrannical chauvinistic patriarchal society mature as a feminist is very interesting and fascinating. Shobha De uses her novels as a medium of expression of the new reality of women in our contemporary society. She projects human values to which women in our society are stuck. She projects a positive image of Indian women who refuse to be 'Sati-Savitri' brand or stereotype of women dependent on patriarchal males in every domain.

Shobha De is popularly known as a fashion model and a celebrity writer; she emerged as a famous novelist within a short span of her life. She has published several works, *Socialite Evenings*, *Sisters*, *Snapshots*, *Spouse*, *Speed Post*, *Starry Nights*, *Second Thoughts*, *Shooting from the Hips*, *Sultry Days*. Her novels are not a series of bodice ripper but as David Davidar observed, they are serious attempts at discovering India through Indian eyes. Shobha De has been labelled as evergreen queen of pornography, a mart of pulp fiction, a vamp of feministic ideals and experimenter of feminism or a mere peddler of pornographic fiction by her critics. She explores the world of human relationships; she believes in frank narration and concentrates on the problems of women. Her various characters are modern, strong, and they take bold decisions to survive in society which makes her essentially a feminist novelist. Shobha De has raised sexuality as a weapon and as a problem for the women in the traditional Indian society.

In *Socialite Evenings*, Karuna, Anjali and Ritu are the main female characters. Karuna is the narrator of events in the novel beginning from the birth of Karuna in a dusty clinic in a small village of Satara in Maharashtra. They move to Bombay because of her father's transfer. In the novel Karuna the protagonist is the narrator relating the events and experiences of her life. Karuna's initiation into the world of fashion and glamour was assisted by Anjali, wife of an affluent socialite.

Karuna is an ambitious woman whose dream is to become an actress and a celebrity. She has insatiable appetite for sex. She dates ad film-maker whom she believed will recommend her to become an actress. This novel is fraught with feminist agendas and manifestations. Karuna refuses to succumb to the hegemony of male culture. *Socialite Evenings* presents the spectrum of marginalization of Indian women by their husbands and predatory lovers. Karuna marries a rich man whom she expects to make her a celebrity. Karuna realizes that their marriage was an utter failure: "the wrong man for the wrong reasons at the wrong time. Her husband is just the average Indian husband uninspiring, untutored. He was not made for introspection" (65).

Karuna is a rebel towards the attitude of her husband, who is always busy in his monotonous activities like reading business pages from *The Times of India*: "you don't really count, except in the context of my priorities. It was taken for granted that our needs were secondary to theirs and that in same way we ought to be grateful for having a roof over our head and four square meals a day" (69).

In patriarchal society husbands oppresses women by abusing, harassing them mentally, humiliating them as they are meant to undergo the same, but the new feminists of Shobha De's novel never digest or tolerate such treatment. One of the main tenets of feminism is that they are never second, or inferior to the males. Ritu's statement is shattering to the chauvinists: "men like dogs could be conditioned through reward and punishment" (87).

Shobha De paints the male flock, as losing their power of chauvinism, they feel incompetent and trivial. In her characters she portrays the picture of radical libertarian feminist ideology; who believe in the violation of sexual norms, they want to control their sexual aspects. Karuna wants to abort her unborn child reflects the ideology of radical libertarian feminism who favour abortion and use of birth control methods. They don't want to miss promotions and other perks because of their maternity; they are determined to be equated on par with the working men.

Karuna is not happy with her marriage. There is a breakdown of interaction between the couple. She was taken for granted by her husband but Karuna as a radical feminist will never concede defeat or to be dictated by her husband's whims.

Karuna has an illicit affair with Girish, her husband's friend, who satisfies her biological needs. Her husband was busy not attending to her sexual needs. Karuna justifies it and says: "You never cared to understand me as a woman." (185) The modern day women are sexually liberated who freely express their desires and wants. It was her husband who is put to blame not Karuna. Sexual pleasure is not the patent for men only but also for new women.

Anjali in the novel enacts a marriage with Abe and rejoices in orgiastic acrobatics. Having a passion for illimitable sex, she has frequent sex encounters. Her women are after the desire of the body and itching sensation. Karuna also rejects social and religious taboos and enjoys her amorous relationship with Girish. These women symbolize absolute celebration of womanhood with least respect for their married partners. "I felt like an indifferent boarder in the house going through the motions of housekeeping and playing wife but resentment and rebellion remained just under the surface, ready to break out at the smallest provocation" (69)

Karuna no more respects the stereotype role of women. Shobha De's vamp ideology of feminine is an escape to attain individuality and break free from the patriarchal shackles of marriage, motherhood and traditional bondages.

Shobha De's women like Karuna, Anjali and Ritu project their passions by female power play in order to defuse the male ego. They like to be eroticized as objects and view themselves as erotic objects, not subjects. Ritu exploits her sexual breakthrough, her female potential to keep her husband within her reach and within her control. Ritu tells Karuna: "make them feel that you have done them a favour by marrying them . . . make them feel insecure. Let them think you'll walk out on them if they don't toe the line. That's what keeps them in their place" (86)

Shobha De is exploring the ideology of sexual power politics of the feminine as an instrument to control men. Karuna's mother prefers the traditional way of life which is safe and moral and respectable unlike sexual amorous life with no future, health or security. She wants Karuna to marry and be subservient to her husband, who will be her protector and saviour. But Karuna questions: "but mother why does security rest with a man? I feel confident now that I can look after myself. I am earning as much money as any man, I have a roof over my head I don't really have any responsibility. I am at peace with myself. I am not answerable to anyone. . . . I can't make my sacrifices—not now." (276) The above statement shatters the basic patriarchal dogma that which identifies man's role as the head of the family, master, bread-winner, and as the protector of family. Shobha De's women also symbolize 'Socialist feminists,' who fundamentally believe in financial liberty for women, Karuna testifies that woman without influence of man can fulfil her responsibilities and have a social and economic standing in the society. The modern day urban women are competent, confident and independent they identify themselves with ideology of socialist feminism. The above statements of Karuna are the quintessence of socialist feminist ideology. The novel adores the feminine consciousness of her characters.

The novel *Sisters* is set in world of business tycoons, wicked, egoist, and womanizers who are anti-feminists. Mikki (Mallika) the protagonist inherits her father's industry as her parents die in an air crash. Alisha is her step-sister by her father's concubine, who is not accepted by the family. Mikki as a new feminist dons the role of a company head. Her industry was bankrupt; hence she borrows money from her fiancée Navin. When Navin's mother learns about it their engagement is cancelled. Binny's middle-aged businessman, a womanizer, baits her, and promises to lend financial support. He lures her into bed and marries her. Both the sisters in the novel, Mikki and Alisha, are sexually exploited by the patriarchal males. Alisha is sexually exploited by Dr. Kurien and Navin.

In Shobha De's novels marriage is bondage, they break from their bondage and lead an independent life. Whereas Mikki surrenders to Binny and genuinely loves him they enter into wedlock and thereafter, she loses liberty and he turns her into a domestic woman yearning for her husband's love and affection. Binny marginalizes her and suppresses her; her property is transferred to Binny: "willing to compromise her own life, if it meant he'd notice her, listen to her, acknowledge her existence." (140)

He denies her motherhood for she was to keep always fit for him. Mikki loses her power of feminism. Mikki displays the qualities of the cultural feminists who believe in feminine qualities viz., patience, endurance, merciful, sacrificing and other traits. Mikki's situation in the novel throws light on the harsh realities of the patriarchal society in urban modern day rich class society dominated by males. Mikki is constantly at war with herself as a woman and a human being. She failed to find a man in Binny with whom she could confide. Binny, suspecting her chastity, turns her out of his home. She pleads innocence and tells him. "Binny . . . I love you only you. . . . I can't live without you." (141)

Binny had a concubine and children by her; he wanted divorce from Mikki. Binny and his concubine and his children die in a car accident, thereafter Mikki receives his father's industry as well as Binny's property. Her experience with Binny gives an insight into her being as a woman, as an individual and from innocence to maturity she transforms. This also hints at the growing awareness among the women who begin to rise from the eternal slumber and call shots. In one of the passages, Mikki asserts: "thank you for your advice, Ramankaka. I appreciate and value your words. But I'd like you to have few of mine now. I can't change my sex . . . but can change most about everything else . . . this is going to be my show and I intend running it on my own terms." (430) Shobha De presents in this passage that new women as entrepreneurs and workaholics they can compete with their male counterparts, they are successful and efficient in any of the given sectors.

Ironically Mikki and Alisha unite at the end of the novel. Mikki did what his father was afraid to do, she acknowledges that Alisha is her step-sister. Breaking the norms and rigidities maintained by patriarchal hypocrites in the society. Shobha De ends the novel with victory for the feminists. She personifies Mikki, though at the outset of the novel she is marginalized and loses her identity and power by leading a life of subjugation under the umbrella protection of the patriarchal male. From weakness and exploitation, she rises and matures as liberated socialist feminist.

Shobha De uses her novels as medium of expression of the new reality of women in contemporary society. She projects human values to which women in our society are stuck. She is with polemical feministic ideology but strongly influenced by feministic consciousness through the novels of *Socialite Evenings* and *Sisters*. She projects a positive image of urban Indian women who refuse to be stereotype women, dependent on patriarchal males in every domain. Her characters Karuna, Mikki and Alisha depict modern-day neo-feminists who are liberated from the clutches of patriarchal society. They are liberated economically and sexually and are equated with the western feminists. Shobha De projects her characters losing identity, freedom and significance because of the norms and beliefs of marriage which makes her heroines confined and marginalized by patriarchal system. Hence we see a sea of change taking places in her female characters once they break free from rigid patriarchal notions and social norms. They don't have faith in marriage; marriage is nominal for these characters. They indulge in sexual affairs outside wedlock and identify with radical libertarian feminists. Shobha De also depicts women who believe in working and are not dependant on males; they are stronger financially. Thus Shobha De in her novels portrays feministic ideologies in different shades and colours; her motto is to eradicate the sexism or gender-related oppression on the women. Therefore it is not incorrect or exaggeration to state that her novel fights for women liberties, women empowerment, and indeed celebrates feminism.

Works Cited

De, Shobha, *Socialite Evenings* (New Delhi: Penguin 1990).

_____. *Sisters* (New Delhi: Penguin, 1992).

Beauvoir, Simone de, *The Second Sex,* trans. H.M. Parshley (London: Penguin 1974).

Tong, Rosemarie, *Feminist Thought* (London: Routledge, 1993).

Ramachandran, Janki, *"Survival Tactics," The Hindu*, Feb. 2, 1997.

Chandra, Subhash, "Family and Marriage in Shobha De's *Socialite Evenings*,"

French, Marilyn, *Beyond Power on Women, Men and Morals* (New York: Summit 1985).

Indu in *Roots and Shadows* and Saru in *The Dark Holds No Terrors*: A Comparative Study

M. SRILAKSHMI
Aditya Engineering College, Surampalem, Kakinada

The part of the Indian society most affected by the changes around is woman. So a wide range of women characters occupy the fictional province of Indian writing. With feminine sensibility, sensitivity and understanding, women writers represent the contemporary Indian woman with all her longings, aspirations and frustrations. The fullest expression of women problems are displayed through the various themes in the novels of Shashi Deshpande who has probed into the female persona and focused on perceiving the perplexities of life and the protagonist's status in it. The protagonists Indu and Saru, in the novels *Roots and Shadows* (1983) and *The Dark Holds No Terrors* (1980) respectively, mark the beginning of the quest of woman. They are presented as the women who are free from the limitations of the society, culture, nature and their own fear and guilt. Indu and Saru oppose the traditional way of life, its rituals, ceremonies, and family values.

The journeys of Indu and Saru begin with an unorthodox marriage leading to the problems of adjustment and alienation. Indu and Saru oppose the structuring of men and women in gendered roles which restrict their freedom and potential. They struggle to adjust to these restrictive and moulded roles. Both the protagonists, at the stage of rejection, pause at some point in their adult roles as wife and mother, and take a long, careful look at their childhood and adolescence. Interconnecting these two phases of youth and adulthood, Deshpande has provided a new insight into their lives as women within a particular society. Past events influence the lives of the protagonists and these events gain meaning by what happens in the present. Deshpande uses the technique of flashback as both the novels begin with the protagonists returning to their parents' home. The conflict in them is resolved through their despondent unconscious surrender to traditional roles. Marriage, which they think makes them free, on contrary proves to be another trap totally restricting their freedom. Despite enormous sacrifices at the professional level, marriage obstructs the growth of these protagonists as individuals. Marriage is viewed as dark rooms where terror awaits. They try to escape from one trap but unfortunately and unknowingly they get caught in another trap which they realize only after marriage. Even the enlightened and educated Indu is forced to be flaccid and insensitive, cautiously veiling her true feelings from Jayant who remains a conservative partner expecting his wife to play a meek role. Saru-Manu marriage turns bitter because of sexual sadism originating from professional jealousy. The professional growth of Saru gradually deteriorates as Manu tries to conquer by sexual assaults.

The marital relationships of Saru and Indu fade and falter due to silence. The role of a passive wife makes Indu discontented and silent. Indu's husband Jayant believes that fervour makes a woman unwomanly and wishes Indu to be passive even in the sexual act. This silence creates a crevice between Indu and Jayant. Silence makes Saru's relationship with her husband complex and there is no exaggeration in saying that it is lack of proper communication that has created all the problems. All perplexity in Saru's life might have resolved if she had tried to come out of her silence by talking to her husband.

Both Saru and Indu go through disillusionment in sex and suffer a silent sexual humiliation. Their sexual situation forces these women to extramarital relationships which mark their paths to individuation. One important aspect to be recorded with regard to these extra-marital relationships is that neither Indu nor Saru reflect a sense of guilt. Saru's illicit affair with Boozie also does not lead to sexual contentment. Indu's relationship with Naren has a totally different magnitude. They experience a sense of sexual independence freeing themselves from sexual politics. Further, these heroines arrive at a realistic view of love as physical instinct.

In the lives of Saru and Indu, mother-daughter alienation is marked and it creates hatred towards womanhood in general. This hatred arises from their graceless initiation to womanhood and the constant reminder of their inferiority to the male. The recurrent words of Kamala, Saru's mother "You're growing up" and "You're a woman now" (*The Dark,* 62) caution her and hamper her movements. This develops in Saru a deep hatred for her mother which remains a part of herself and turns her into a rebel. The rift between Saru and her mother, which destroys both her childhood and adult life, is felt throughout the novel. Love of a mother boosts the morale of a girl and at the same time rejection makes her rootless just like Saru. The clash between Saru and her mother typifies the clash between the old and the new; the traditional and the modern. Saru feels that her mother is a stumbling block for her freedom and revolts against her by marrying Manohar. Motherless Indu doesn't succeed in establishing rapport with the dominating Akka because she reflects authority. Indu marries Jayant in rebellion against the family, particularly Akka. Revolt and escape from the restrictions imposed by the parental homes ends in another catastrophe. It is evident that it is not love that binds them in marriage but refusal to accept their failure. So in their journeys, both Saru and Indu have no mothers who as role models could have given them a bright future.

The societies in which Saru and Indu live painfully reflected gender bias. Real social change is impossible unless men wish to accept the change. It is the environment that decides the attitude of the girl child where her personality develops through upbringing and socialization. Saru is a victim of gender discrimination which ultimately leads to sibling jealousy and her involuntary involvement in the drowning of her brother. Death of the son ruins Saru's mother forever and she continues to live with that loss for the rest of her life. She refuses to forgive her daughter Saru for having created that loss. Saru receives neither love nor affection and fails to conquer that sentiment. Human attachments fail to help her in the later stages. The guilty conscience created by the baseless blame of the mother blisters her mind. The secondary place attributed to women in the family makes Indu a rebel. Certain rights which only men enjoyed like having tea served in their rooms, which the women never enjoyed influence Indu. As a girl she was always told to be obedient and unquestioning and accept everything, even defeat with grace. She doesn't accept this discrimination and this unwillingness brings out the rebellious side of her nature.

The protagonists Saru and Indu rebel against their socially imposed roles as they get overburdened. They symbolically journey to the past by visiting their family. The journey helps them to analyze their relationships and assess themselves as imperfect individuals. The temporary withdrawal helps them to understand their own contribution to their distress. They realize that living up to the expectations of others has led to loss of identity. They have been compelled to seek identity by continuous approval and recognition from others. This experience enables them to finally accept that there is selfhood in being a wife, a sister, a mother, and a career woman. The return to their families of orientation which they left in rebellion against maternal authority itself is a part of the process of compromise. The return home helps them to release themselves from emotional bondage.

Saru undergoes the difficult journey into her 'self' and learns to free herself of guilt, shame and humiliation. She recognizes her own role in damaging many of her relations due to her sense of fear, guilt and self-accusation. Later with the words of her father she realizes her social role and prepares to face the world and her husband. Indu liberates herself from the shadows of the past and gains strength to resign her job. From an individual without an identity, she matures into an individual with her own identity. She decides to build up her life on love and honesty. Both Saru and Indu pass through five phases in their lives, i.e., rebellion against the patriarchal norms, escape through marriage, frustration, return to parental homes and ultimately an attempt to consolidate. They step back to the maternal homes with a marked change. They attain identity through their own efforts. Their painful and suppressed struggle ends with assertion of their individuality. They begin to change their lives through vigilance, courage, self-analysis and self-understanding. Conquering their fears, reconciling with the past and understanding the need of bonding they achieve harmony in life. Ultimately, they understand, adjust and without sacrificing their individuality they decide to begin a new, honest life.

Works Cited

Bala, Suman. ed. *Women in the Novels of Shashi Deshpande.* New Delhi: Khosla, 2001.

Barnes, Anjali. Comparative Study of Shashi Deshpande's and Anita Nair's Feminism. *Global Journal of Human Social Science*, 11:4.

Bhavani, J. "Is Shashi Deshpande a Feminist?" *Literary Journal*, 2.2, 1992-93.

Deshpande, Shashi. *The Dark Holds No Terrors.* New Delhi: Vikas, 1980.

_____. *Roots and Shadows.* Hyderabad: Orient Longman, 1983.

Dhawan, R.K., ed. *Feminism and Recent Indian Literature.* 2 Vols. New Delhi: Prestige, 2008.

_____. *Indian Women Novelists*. 18 Vols. New Delhi: Prestige, 1995.

Indramohan, T.M.J. *Shashi Deshpande: A Critical Spectrum.* New Delhi: Atlantic, 2004.

Kavya, B. "Marital Rape in Shashi Deshpande's Fiction." *Indian Streams Research Journal*, 2: IV, 2012.

Mala, R. "The Predicament of the Indian Woman: The Heroines in the Novels of Shashi Deshpande: A Select Study." M. Phil. Dissertation, Pondicherry University, 1989.

Narayan, Shyamala A. "Shashi Deshpande." *Contemporary Novelists*. 1991.

Philoni, Maria A. Sr. and Shanthi. "Awakening of Spiritual Intelligence in the Women Protagonist of Shashi Deshpande and its Significance in Life," *Journal of Teaching and Research in English Literature,* 2:3, 2011.

Prakash, Ravindra. "Becoming a Whole: A Reading of Shashi Deshpande's *The Dark Holds No Terrors*." *Language Forum*, 18.1,1992.

Ramachandra, Ragini. Review of Shashi Deshpande's *The Dark Holds No Terrors. The Literary Criterion,* 21: 1 and 2, 1986.

Sandhu, Sarabjit. *The Image of Woman in Shashi Deshpande.* New Delhi: Prestige, 1991.

Sebastian, Mrinalini. *The Novels of Shashi Deshpande in Postcolonial Arguments.* New Delhi: Prestige, 1997.

Shanthi, S.M. "An Interview with Shashi Deshpande." Tradition Versus Modernity in the Novels of Shashi Deshpande, An unpublished M. Phil Dissertation, Madurai Kamaraj University, April 1989, 2.

Sharma, Siddharth. *Shashi Deshpande's Novel: A Feminist Study.* New Delhi: Atlantic, 1989.

Sisodiya, Suraj Sing. *Shashi Deshpande*. New Delhi: Prestige.

Arundhati Roy's Exotic Images of the Indian Setting in *The God of Small Things*

HALIMAH MOHAMED ALI
Universiti Sains Malaysia

Why has a novel like *The God of Small Things* (1997) that deals with issues that are indigenously Indian dominated the Western literary market and scene? It could be argued that the 1997 Booker Prize gave *The God of Small Things* more authenticity and pulled it into the centre of the world literary market, which is obviously dominated by the West. Nevertheless, there might be more to it. Ziauddin Sardar argues: "In postmodernism, marginality takes centre-stage as western culture discovers Otherness and its own ethnocentric perspectives" (1998:12). In the novel the caste system, which is indigenously Indian, the Indian landscape and its people are central. Thus, it presents to the West the Otherness that Sardar touches upon, and this presentation holds up the ethnocentric bias that the West has generated and believed of the Other i.e. Indian.

The novel has many themes. They encompass caste and untouchability within the Ayemenem society, the failure of Christianity and Marxism to fulfil the aspirations and dreams of the Untouchables, social prejudices based on religion and caste, lack and loss of individual liberty, the love affair between an Untouchable man and a high caste woman and the deterioration of

India, its culture and its people. This paper will discuss them vis-à-vis the discussion of the setting that is presented in the fiction.

The analysis will be carried out based on the overriding issue of how this postmodernist fiction extends a Western Orientalist framework. In discussing this I will employ theories put forward by Edward Said and Sardar mainly. Amartya Sen's notion of the exoticist approach and the magisterial approach will also be applied in my analysis. Dipankar Gupta's argument of how India is undergoing social and political change though it is far from modern will be employed to discuss the presentation of the caste system as well as issues of hybridity and mimicry. I will also discuss the author's act of pandering to the West i.e. the Western market. Frantz Fanon is another important figure that will be referred to in this reading. He will be used to analyze the mimic and hybrid characters, and also to postulate that *The God of Small Things* is an extension of Orientalism. It will be argued that Orientalism from within the Indian landscape and psyche is rendered via the novel. Overall the aim of this paper is to establish the way in which this postmodernist novel has been influenced by Orientalist ideas and frameworks, and how it extends them.

The God of Small Things is a postmodernist fiction. This is due to the fact that it adheres to the classic postmodernist formula. The story is non-linear, it has no closure, and it is dark as well as bleak, filled with chaos. It begins when Estha and Rahel are thirty-one. The narration is non-linear as it jumps from the present to the past and vice versa. Sometimes past and present are fused together that unless we are careful, the details can be confusing. While ASB is framed by two marriages *The God of Small Things* is encased between two different eras, the present and the past. The story starts with Rahel's return to Ayemenem from America and ends in the past, where Ammu, her mother says goodbye to Velutha, her Untouchable lover.

Another postmodern element is that it is bleak and filled with chaos. India is shown as a country that is ugly and backward. It is filled with people who are either caricatures or inept and lazy. There is no happy ending for the characters. They either die or live colourless and empty lives.

The ending of the novel has no closure, which is typical of a postmodernist text. The final chapter depicts the Velutha-Ammu affair, that marks the end of her children's happiness and stability. It ends with Ammu saying goodbye to Velutha at the river bank, the first night after their affair begins.

This paper discusses the setting that makes India exotic and a stereotype. The main setting is Ayemenem, a village in the state of Kerala in India. In the fiction, it is a model of a much larger India. The setting is like a stage where the action takes place within set perimeters. Outside or off that stage nothing is real. Places outside Ayemenem and Kerala are mentioned; Australia, the tea estate, Canada, Trivandrum, Delhi, New York but they are not described in detail as Ayemenem is and they do not come to life as this small village across which a river called Meenachal runs. The foreign locations as well as Trivandrum, a small city in India, are only pictured as places where some of the characters migrate to in order to escape Ayemenem.

Though Ayemenem is not a fictitious locale, the author has only changed the spelling, which is actually Aymanam,1 she has actualized a world and filled it up with characters that she has created. They have been set against Western ideals of ethical behaviour, social equality, democracy, prosperity and others that will be illustrated in this paper. However, in the small Ayemenem community which is depicted, a family of Syrian Christians: the Ipes, the Untouchables, the Touchable workers in the family's factory, the local Marxist leader and the Touchable policemen, the lack of Western morals are highlighted. Though this paper concentrates on the setting of the novel, it will also discuss how characters are depicted within it and also the thematic concerns of the novel, because they are interrelated.

The God of Small Things provides for its readers a 'knowledge' of India and a glimpse into the Indian life from their Western living rooms or libraries as they sit and read the novel. From the start, the act of Othering India is already at work. The detailed description of the weather and landscape sets the country apart from the West and provides for the readers an exotic location that is far away from their homes and libraries.

First, let us observe how the weather and the vegetation are used to exoticize the locale. The readers are introduced to Ayemenem vis-à-vis the weather. The novel begins with: "May in Ayemenem is a hot, brooding month. The days are long and humid. The river shrinks and black crows gorge on bright mangoes in still, dustgreen trees. Red bananas ripen. Jackfruits burst. Dissolute bluebottles hum vacuously in the fruity air. Then they stun themselves against windowpanes and die, fatly baffled in the sun." (1)

Through the weather and the vegetation we are introduced to the extraordinary India. It is rendered Other to the West. Words like "hot," "mangoes," "bananas" and "Jackfruits," a universal hallmark of Asia, pronounce this othering. Where else can one find mangoes, bananas and jackfruits if not in hot and mostly sunny Asia? Mangoes are a trademark of India since the country is well known for its luscious and sweet mangoes that are exported throughout the world. Though in *The God of Small Things* mangoes are not given much emphasis, there are novelists who have used this fruit to give their fiction a more local flavour. In Vikram Seth's *A Suitable Boy* (1991), Mrs. Rupa Mehra, a diabetic, cannot live without eating mangoes when they are in season. Another Indian writer who has used this exotic fruit is David Davidar in his novel titled *The House of Blue Mangoes* (2002). Another unusual reference in the excerpt above is "red bananas." We are all familiar with yellow and green bananas, but we do not associate the colour red with bananas. The red bananas make India doubly mysterious in the minds of Western readers: After the hot weather of Ayemenem, we are shown the monsoons. These are also synonymously Asia:

> By June the south-west monsoon breaks and there are three months of wind and water with short spells of sharp, glittering sunshine that thrilled children snatch to play with. The countryside turns an immodest green. Boundaries blur as tapioca fences take root and bloom. Brick walls turn mossgreen. Pepper vines snake up electric poles. Wild creepers burst through laterite banks and spill across the flooded roads. Boats ply in the bazaars. And small fish appear in the puddles that fill the PWD potholes on the highways. (1)

We are introduced to images that are both beautiful and ugly. With the rain comes the luscious greenery that is seen everywhere, in tapioca fences, brick walls that are covered with moss, on poles and in drains where creepers grow. But the monsoon also brings about floods. The potholes that are filled with puddles on the highway spoils the initial beauty in the description. The image created is that though India is beautiful it is not well taken care of by the people. This similar picture is drawn in other places too, as will be demonstrated later. The description above symbolizes the uncontrolled growth and fecundity of India. Though it is green and beautiful, there is wilderness about it. The growth is overpowering and unmanageable. It is another face of India that the Westerner will declare as familiar.

The novel has been placed in an exotic setting that is attractive to the international public. Its historical and cultural diversity is also an attraction. According to Saadia Toor:

> *The God of Small Things* is set in Kerala, a state whose multi-layered cultural heritage—a result of centuries of interaction with Arab and Chinese tradesman, Jews, Syrian Christians, Dutch and British colonizers—its tropical climate, and its as-yet-unspoilt natural beauty, is 'Other' even for most Indians. As a testimony to its potential as marketable commodity within India, it should be noted

> that, over the past couple of years, it has featured on tourism shows made by and for Indians, broadcast over satellite television, and it has been the chosen locale for an Indian remake of Laura Esquivel's Like Water for Chocolate, telecast as a serial over the India-based but Rupert Murdoch owned television network Star TV. (19)

In light of Toor's argument it will be illustrated that Kerala's diverse cultural heritage and history is utilized to the fullest. This in turn makes the writing exotic and marketable in the West. As a native Roy capitalizes on Kerala, her land of birth, and creates a fascinating piece of work like *The God of Small Things*. The approach that is used in her fiction is mostly exoticist. Sen states the exoticist approach "concentrates on the wondrous aspects of India" and focuses on "what is different, what is strange" (28). This analysis will draw out how the Othered and exotic India is depicted.

The description of the surroundings is striking and enchanting, as well as explicit. The "unspoilt natural beauty" that Toor suggests is obvious. In the example below the Touchable policemen are walking towards the History House in their search for Velutha. The jungle that they walk through is described:

> They trudged past darter birds on the top of trees, drying their sodden wings spread out like laundry against the sky. Past egrets. Cormorants. Adjutant storks. Sarus cranes looking for space to dance. Purple herons with pitiless eyes. Deafening, their *wraakwraakwraak*. Motherbirds and their eggs. . . . Beyond the swamp that smelled of still water, they walked past ancient trees cloaked in vines. Gigantic mani plants. Wild pepper. Cascading purple acuminus. (305)

Again we are brought face to face with luscious vegetation, but this time to add to the exotica, birds are introduced. The image that is created is beautiful. Imagine a bird drying its wings against the sky. This is a lovely and exotic sight. In this limited excerpt we are flooded with the pictures of the different kinds of birds that can be seen in the jungle of Ayemenem. This jungle is a heaven for bird watchers and bird enthusiasts. The listings above give an expression of certainties. The timelessness of India is emphasized. They signify a diverse, composite as well as a complete picture of unchanging life. The readers are presented with things that are familiar and unfamiliar, known yet not known. However, outside this fictional setting how likely would it be for us to come across all these birds in a matter of minutes just as we take a walk through the jungle, and the Ayemenem jungle is not vast.

How realistic and believable is the description? *The God of Small Things* being a postmodernist novel, we have to refer to Sardar's second principle of postmodernism "the denial of Reality" (1998: 9). His argument is that in postmodernism "we see . . . what we want to see" due to the lack of "ultimate reality" (9). His third principle of postmodernism also applies in this context. Due to the fact that there is no reality the world is a "simulacrum" where "all distinction between image and material reality has been lost" (10). His argument is that "All social life is . . . regulated not by reality but by simulations, models, pure images and representations" (10). The reality that we see in the excerpt above is thus the creation of the author. Though it is imagined, it seems quite authentic if you are reading about it from a distance and are unfamiliar with the locale. For the Western reader, the distance is quite great and to most, the location is alien.

Why have the facts been embellished? Again I refer to Sardar who says: "The indigenous knowledge of the Others, along with their history, is now being appropriated on an unprecedented scale to become consumer fodder for the West, to be recycled and exported back to non-western cultures" (1998: 14). The truth has been embroidered because this is what the West wants from indigenous writers. The author is in a position to do this because she has local knowledge of Kerala and Ayemenem, enhancing the authenticity of her rendition.

We are also introduced to Cochin, another town in the state of Kerala. We see it in passing through the eyes of the twins, Estha and Rahel. However, this picture lacks the luscious greenery of India. The images that the readers are fed with are of degeneration, laziness and the backwardness of the fictional society.

The car that the twins are travelling in with their uncle Chacko, their mother Ammu and their grand aunt Baby Kochamma to Cochin has to stop at a railway crossing. Within this short interval of their journey we are again bombarded with images of India that are exotic and stereotypical. First of all we see Murlidharan, a man who has degenerated mentally as well as physically through the years:

> Murlidharan, the level crossing lunatic, perched cross-legged and perfectly balanced on the milestone. . . . Murlidharan was naked except for the plastic bag that somebody had fitted onto his head like a transparent chef's cap. . . . He couldn't remove his cap even if he wanted to because he had no arms. They had been blown off in Singapore in '42, within the first week of his running away from home to join the fighting ranks of the Indian National Army. After Independence he had himself registered as a Grade I Freedom Fighter and had been allotted a free-first class railway pass for life. This too he had lost (along with his mind), so he could no longer live on trains or in refreshment rooms in railway stations. (62-63)

We see a man who has lost his mind, thus he cannot take care of himself. This madman has no arms, which makes it more difficult for him to be presentable. A man who does not have the power to take off a plastic bag that someone has put on his head cannot be expected to put on clothes. By creating an armless lunatic, Roy doubly exoticizes this figure. This is an example of the stereotype of the Other that has been rampant in Orientalist discourse as argued by Fanon and Said. Fanon postulates that the stereotype of the White man about the Negro remains (1970: 83). Said's argument on this issue indicates that the West that controls the media, print as well as electronic, swallow the marginal and minority voices. The pictures of the Other that are provided for the world are dominantly negative (Said 1993: 32). The East has always been viewed by the West as helpless, and the character of Murlidharan shows the Other at his ultimate powerlessness. The image is bizarre, also grotesque and humorous. To understand why this stereotype is maintained, we have to refer to Fanon's theory. He argues that the stereotype of the other remains because of the fixed expectations of the West (Fanon 1970: 27). Said and Fanon indicate that the West does not want the image of the Orient that it created via Orientalism to change. However, the era of postcolonialism refrains the West from directly ascribing negative pictures to the East. Instead, writers like Roy become the carriers of Orientalism because they aim for fame and fortune.

Through the window of the car we view an India and Indians that are ironically portrayed. Again via the twins we see the world outside of the car: "An ambulance that said Sacred Heart Hospital was full of a party of people on their way to a wedding. The bride was staring out of the back window, her face partially obscured by the flaking paint of the huge red cross" (60). It is bizarre that an ambulance that is supposed to be used for medical emergencies is ferrying a wedding party. This is another hackneyed image of the Other that is regurgitated. By the misuse of the ambulance the message that goes out to the reader is that Indians are not scrupulous and things are not put to proper use. This is another strange and embarrassing illustration. The nation is shown as a land of extremes, either it is hilarious or it is dark. The European idea of Orientalist backwardness that Said refers to can be detected here. According to Said, Orientalism sustains the binary oppositions of the West and East and the cultural hegemony of the West has given Orientalism the strength that it has today. European culture is hegemonic and viewed as superior to non-European peoples and cultures because Orientalism has fed the idea of a superior European identity to the world. European ideas of Oriental backwardness also reiterate European superiority via Orientalism (Said 1978: 7). The picture of India where its people do not know how to use things restates European supremacy, because a Western reader will of course compare the situation with incidents in his/her own country. The probability of an ambulance being used for a wedding, in England or in America would be very slim unless there was a medical emergency. The author is providing for her readers Orientalism from within.

At the railway crossing we also see a slow moving India. More curious pictures are supplied:

> Initially, when the level crossing had just closed, the Air was full of impatient sound of idling engines. But when the man that manned the crossing came out of his booth, on his backward bending legs and signalled with his limp, flapping walk to the tea stall that they were for a long wait, the drivers switched off their engines and milled about, stretching their legs. With a desultory nod of his bored and sleepy head, the level Crossing divinity conjured up beggars with bandages, men with trays selling pieces of fresh coconut, parippuvadas on banana leaves. And cold drinks. Coca-cola, Fanta, rose-milk. A leper with soiled bandages begged at the car window. 'That looks like Mercurochrome to me,' Ammu said, of his inordinately bright blood. (61)

The image that is created here is that the railway service runs at a leisurely phase. This is a typical impression of Third World countries in Orientalist discourses. The Other's lack of concern for time is declared by Rudyard Kipling in *Kim*. He states: "All hours of the twenty-four are alike to Orientals, and their passenger traffic is regulated accordingly" (Kipling 38). Phrases like "limp, flapping walk" and "bored and sleepy head," create a picture of a country and society that are idle and sluggish. This image enhances the myth of the lazy native that has been projected by many Orientalist discourses about the natives of colonized lands. S.H. Alatas in his book *The Myth of the Lazy Native* confronted this stereotype that the West has constructed of the Other. However, he concentrated on the natives of Malaysia, Indonesia and the Philippines. In the case of Malaysia, according to Alatas, this myth was created by the British colonizers, because the Malay refused to be "a tool in the production system of the British colonial capitalism" (72). The slow moving India that is presented in *The God of Small Things* is a legacy of the colonial past that has taken root in the consciousness of the Other. The author, an Indian elite, is best described using D. Gupta's theory that labels the upper classes of India as "Orientalist" products (17). I have maintained that the Indian-English writers are 'children of the West.' Thus, like Western Orientalists who used the magisterial approach to devalue the natives and render them as inferior, Roy too has employed a similar method.

The cliché of the lying native is hinted at when Ammu points out that the blood on the leper's bandages looks like mercurochrome. Kipling also shows the Oriental/Indian as untrustworthy. There are pictures of Indians who cheat and lie in *Kim*, and Kim is said to be able to "lie like an Oriental" (34). These Western prejudices of the Other that still exist today are reiterated by native writers. D. Gupta argues that the West would rather pay the Oriental to Other and debase his/her people, country and culture because of the political correct notions that exist today (18-21). The West that has shown itself to be concerned about humanity and human rights would easily be labelled as racist, dogmatic or hypocrite if it unambiguously provided negative pictures of the East, though that is still its view. When the image of a listless and languid country is shown, the West is presented with the picture that they want of the Other.

Apart from the stereotype there is also exotica in the passage above. At the level crossing as the people prepare for a long wait, beggars, hawkers selling local delicacies and cold drinks as well as a leper emerge out of nowhere. We are informed that these people are "conjured up" by the "level Crossing divinity." Sen's theory of the exoticist approach that "concentrates on the wondrous aspects of India" and focuses on "what is different, what is strange" (28) is applicable in this context. The image that is created by the statements "conjured up" and "level Crossing divinity" is of something supernatural. It seems to suggest that all the beggars, the hawkers and the leper emerged through magic. This image of India that is strange and mythical is not new because it has been portrayed in Orientalist writings. Today the magical and the strange in India are delivered for Western consumption by native writers like Roy.

The journey in the car from Ayemenem to Cochin is taken to meet and bring to Ayemenem Margaret Kochamma, Chacko's ex-wife who is English and their daughter Sophie Mol. At Cochin airport we again see clichéd and outrageous as well as colourful impressions of India.

There is the picture of the filthy and dirty native. We are told: "Red betel spit stains spattered their kangaroo stomachs like fresh wounds" (138). The kangaroos are actually dustbins that are shaped as kangaroos. We are shown filth, lack of hygiene, and lack of manners or decency in India and of Indians via the description of the dustbins that are spat on. An airport is a place where one is first introduced to a country or place. Therefore, whatever we see will form our impression of the place and its people. Again the binary opposition that has been created since Orientalism is at work here. As Fanon has put it: "Sin is Negro as virtue is white" (1970: 98). This indicates that the other is viewed in a negative light. In this case filth is India and Indians and cleanliness is the West and Westerners. This is a picture that a Western reader will have in his/her mind. To understand something that is alien to us we occasionally compare it to something that is familiar. A reader living in London will of course have the well-known image of Heathrow Airport in his mind. Of course there will be no betel spit stains on the dustbins there.

Therefore, the binary oppositions of the self and the Other become active in the reader's mind.

Through the airport, the image of India is drawn for the readers in small doses. This novel is not an epic—unlike the famous Indian classic *Mahabharata* that is vast or Seth and Mistry's novels that have been described as epics of India in many internet sources. Yet, they are well presented, and they succeed in Othering and exoticizing India. For example:

> The arrivals lounge was a press of love and eagerness, because the Bombay-Cochin flight was the flight that all the Foreign Returnees came home on. The families had come to meet them. From all over Kerala. On long bus journeys. From Ranni, from Kumili, from Vizhinjam, from Uzhavoor. Some of them had camped at the airport overnight, and had brought their food with them. And tapioca chips and chackkavelaichathu for the way back. They were all there—the deaf ammoomas, the cantankerous, arthritic appoopans, the pining wives, scheming uncles, children with the runs. The fiancées to be reassessed. The teacher's husband still waiting for his Saudi visa. The teacher's husband's sisters waiting for their dowries. The wire bender's pregnant wife [and] . . . a mother not wanting to give up her Good Place near the railing, aimed her distracted baby's penis into an empty bottle while he smiled and waved at the people around him. (138)

Exotica is delivered to us via names of places that are mentioned: "Ranni," "Kumili," Vizhinjam" and "Uzhavoor." Some of these names are difficult to pronounce and they are unfamiliar to foreigners. These are not big cities like Bombay or Delhi but small villages or towns in Kerala. Food is another means used to exoticize the narrative. Tapioca chips and chackkavelaichathu are mentioned. Foreign audience may be able to visualize tapioca chips by picturing potato chips but chackkavelaichathu cannot be imagined since the language is alien for the reader. Though a semi-familiar image is created when tapioca chips are introduced, India and her people are Othered with the labelling of the other food item in Malayalee.

The natives are also rendered different via their names. There are "deaf ammoomas" and "cantankerous, arthritic appoopans." A reader who is unfamiliar with Malayalee will interpret them to be old people because they have ailments that normally affect the elderly. These are also familial terms expressing specific standing of the people, which are unfamiliar to the foreign reader. However, the description of the people at the airport is not a flattering one. Indians appear to be awkward as well as uncivilized. The crude Indian is introduced through the woman who makes her son urinate in an empty bottle. The depiction of how the people at the airport are waiting for their relatives reminds us of people who have gone to watch a football match. It is obvious that just for the sake of exotica stereotype Indians are presented to the readers. The narrative also passes judgement on them. We see the people via Baby Kochamma's gaze and she labels them as "sweeper class" (138). Her thoughts indicate that they are lowly and beneath her, a high caste Syrian Christian.

As Baby Kochamma's critical gaze sweeps across the waiting area of the arrival lounge a distancing of the authorial voice from the everyday Indian occurs. Thus, the act of Othering the natives takes place:

> And there they were, the Foreign Returnees, in wash'n'wear suits and rainbow sunglasses. With an end to grinding poverty in their Aristocrat suitcases. With cement roofs for their thatched houses, and geysers for their parents' bathrooms. With sewage systems and septic tanks. Maxis and high heels. Puff sleeves and lipstick. Mixy-grinders and automatic flashes for their cameras. With keys to count, and cupboards to lock. (140)

The culture that India has of its citizens migrating to other countries to earn their living is mocked. These immigrants are referred to as "The foreign returnees." They are the people who bring back to India the fortune that they earn overseas in order to fulfils their families' dreams of a better future for themselves. By highlighting this aspect the notion of a deficient nation that is unable to sustain its people and their visions is skilfully put forth. The idea that is being postulated is that money from outside is what keeps the Indian and India afloat and gives him/her stability. This suggests that India's resources are not adequate to give the people their basic necessities. By projecting such a view the colonial idea of the inferior Other is strengthened. The Western thought that after independence the Other has lost the progress, modernization, order and stability that the West brought to it is enhanced. What India has attained after independence is poverty as well as a concern with the trappings of what money can buy.

Baby Kochamma's gaze is not the only critical gaze. The optical gaze is the author's. She hides behind the critical eyes of the characters and their criticism of India to pander and cater to the West. India is doubly Othered when the country and fictional characters like Baby Kochamma are portrayed vis-à-vis the ironic view of the characters. As the foreign returnees, minute characters in the novel, lay eyes on the people waiting for them at the airport they feel:

> love and a lick of shame that their families who had come to meet them were so . . . so . . . gawkish. *Look at the way they dressed! Surely they had more suitable airport wear! Why did Malayalees have such awful teeth?* And the airport itself! More like the local bus depot! The birdshit on the building! Oh the spitstains on the kangaroos! *Oho! Going to the dogs India is*. (140)

The gaze of the foreign returnees is filled with criticism. The writer is using an insider-outsider view. She stands apart from her culture and people and judges them. This image, created for the West, authenticates her observation because she is an Indian. Again the picture of the Other that is clichéd and different is delivered to us.

The arguments and examples that have been stated above are best read in light of Sardar's argument about postmodernism's fascination with fiction. According to him, "imagination is the one human frontier that has not been totally colonized; and fiction is the tool that can accomplish this goal" (1998: 175). He argues that the novel can be a very powerful tool that can colonize the imagination and all fictions produce "cultural meanings which are always political meanings" (176). Sardar states that fictions are a "stand-in" for reality, thus through them the Other is shaped and reshaped according to the postmodern desire (176). This postmodern desire that Sardar refers to can also be equated to Western desire since Sardar argues that postmodernism is a Western agenda of neo-colonialism. The less than pleasing pictures of India and its people that we see in *The God of Small Things* can be considered to be the author's bid to pander to the Western agenda of neo-colonialism.

In this section I will discuss how the Ayemenem house is depicted. Rahel's ancestral home is another exotic fixture in the fiction. The idea that India is indeed degenerating is illustrated and emphasized via the residence.

The house is situated on a hill. The family's wealth is depicted via the rubber trees and the paddy fields that surround it. Its pickle factory is also near the house. The house is inherited by Baby Kochamma after Chacko, Rahel's uncle, moves to Canada and Mammachi, her grandmother, dies. Yet what has been given to her is not appreciated. She is more drawn to satellite television and loses interest in everything else including the maintenance of the house. We see the house through Rahel's gaze:

> Filth had laid siege to the Ayemenem house like a medieval army advancing to an enemy castle. It clotted every crevice and clung to the windowpanes. Midges whizzed in teapots. Dead insects lay in empty vases. The floor was sticky. White walls had turned an uneven grey. Brass hinges and doorhandles were dull and greasy to the

> touch. Infrequently used plug points were clogged with grime. Light bulbs had a film of oil on them. The only things that shone were the giant cockroaches that scurried around like varnished go-fers on a film set. (88)

There is also waste, as teapots and empty vases become places where insects live or die in. It shows that things are not being put to their proper use. The filth of the house also mirrors the laziness of their occupants who are also Indians. The lack of initiative and the listings suggest a litany of shared fate of Indian houses generally. The neglect of the house reveals degeneration as well as Indian unhygienic practices.

The unfavourable picture of the Ayemenem house and its occupants is best read using D. Gupta's theory of Westoxication. According to him there are two types of Westoxication, material as well as ideological. In this context it is ideological Westoxication that has influenced the author. According to D. Gupta the Westoxicated Indians adopt Western prejudices without thinking whether they will hurt the country and people because they see themselves as different from the rest of their countrymen (16). He argues that they "pander to petty Western prejudices in the hope that this will win them quick recognition abroad" (16). In Roy's case her novel did succeed in winning the Booker Prize, which led to worldwide fame for the author. This is an example of the reward that she received for pandering and catering to the West.

Even the river Meenachal does not escape from being exoticized. Initially when the twins are children, the river is beautiful. There is a picturesque description of it:

> the coconut trees that bent into it and watched, with coconut eyes, the boats slide by. Upstream in the mornings. Downstream in the evenings. And the dull, sullen sound of the boatmen's bamboo poles as they thudded against the dark, oiled boatwood. It was warm, the water. Greygreen. Like rippled silk. With fish in it. With

> the sky and trees in it. And at night, the broken yellow moon in it. (122-23)

The depiction of the river is romantic and fascinating. The coconut trees are another indication that the setting is Asia, away from Europe and the West. Othering is also done through the diction. The boat in the river is described as "dark" which also symbolizes the Indian who is darker in complexion than the White man. It is also an image of the Orient that has always been seen as dark by the Orientalist. The word echoes Western Orientalist discourses that have described the Other as dirty, black, mysterious and ignorant.

However, the beautiful and romantic image does not remain for long. The initial romantic picture changes with time:

> Years later, when Rahel returned to the river, it greeted her with a ghastly skull's smile, with holes where teeth had been, and a limp hand raised from a hospital bed. Downriver, a saltwater barrage had been built, in exchange for votes from the influential paddy-farmer lobby. The barrage regulated the inflow of saltwater from the backwaters that opened into the Arabian Sea. So now they had two harvests a year instead of one. More rice, for the price of a river. (124)

The tone in the excerpt above is bitter and sarcastic. We are presented with the picture of a river that has lost its beauty and romance via the sick patient metaphor. Indians are judged as unable to appreciate or take care of nature. Politics is also scrutinized. Development, in the context of Kerala, is related to paddy farming, comes for a reason and with a price. The saltwater barrage that is built on the Meenachal river is done by the government in exchange for votes. The farmers get to plant and harvest their paddy twice a year, which means more income for them. However, materialism and modernity have a price; the sacrificial lamb is nature. In the West today there are organizations that are actively fighting to preserve and maintain nature. The degradation of the river Meenachal at the hands of the natives is set against that idea. Thus, the stereotypes that the Other is not sensitive towards his/ her environment and does not know how to take care of the natural assets of his/her country are postulated.

The depiction of the river is read best using Said's theory. According to him the Western view of its own superiority and its image as the saviour of the lesser races is meant to elevate the West (1993: 24). Said argues: "Westerners may have physically left their old colonies in Africa and Asia, but they retained them not only as markets but also as locales on the ideological map over which they continued to rule morally and intellectually" (27). He further argues that this is evident in discourses of those who today "speak for the West and for what the West did as well as for what the rest of the world is, was and may be" (28). Writers like Roy produce Orientalism from within India and Other their people for Western consumption. This is easily done because the West controls the technology and the media.

In this sub-section I will discuss how the History House, a deserted dwelling that stands on the other side of the river from the village, is used to render the fiction exotic. Surrounded by an abandoned rubber estate, it represents the darkest place in Ayemenem and symbolizes India as one of the dark corners of the earth. This image is lifted from the Western stereotype that the East is dark, wicked and horrible, depraved of beauty. Even when the charm of the people and the landscape is highlighted it is taken over by the darkness:

> the house on the other side of the river, in the middle of the abandoned rubber estate where they had never been. Kari Saipu's house. The Black Sahib. The Englishman who had 'gone native.' Who spoke Malayalam and wore mundus. Ayemenem's own Kurtz. Ayemenem his private Heart of Darkness. He had shot himself through the head ten years ago when his young lover's parents had taken the boy away from him and sent him to school. (52)

Intertextual reference is used to give the West the mysteries of the East as well as pictures that are familiar. This part of Ayemenem is compared with Joseph Conrad's fictional setting, the jungle of Congo and its river, in his novel *Heart of Darkness*. *Heart of Darkness*, first published in *Blackwood's Magazine* in Britain between 1898 and 1899 and published as a book in 1902, is a prominent text in the West. It presents a vivid image of the exotic and Othered Africa as it was written at the peak of colonialism. *HOD* is a classic Orientalist discourse that represents the degradation of civilized life in the form of Kurtz. He lives in the jungles of Africa, the Heart of Darkness, and becomes as uncivilized and depraved as the natives that are presented in the novel. By juxtaposing the other side of the river with Kurtz's Heart of Darkness, Roy presents to her Western readers the image of the Other that the West is familiar with since it is acquainted with *Heart of Darkness*. She also conveniently creates a character that resembles Kurtz, the Englishman who turns native whom she names as Kari Saipu, which means Black Sahib. This character is exotic because he represents the white man's fear of turning native.

The above image is of the History House that changes with time. After Rahel returns from America we see another picture of the house. The structure and its surrounding rubber estate are bought by a five-star hotel chain. Turned into a hotel that attracts foreign tourists, it is Othered:

> The view from the hotel was beautiful, but here too the water was thick and toxic. *No Swimming* signs had been put up in stylish calligraphy. They had built a tall wall to screen off the slum and prevent it from encroaching on Kari Saipu's estate. There wasn't much they could do about the smell. (125)

Beauty is ironically juxtaposed with ugliness and foul smell. It is sardonic that the picture of the real India is hidden from the tourists' view. When those who are involved in the tourism camouflage the actual India in order to attract foreigners, truth becomes a simulacrum. I refer to Sardar's theory on postmodernism to explain this. According to him "All social life is . . . regulated not by reality but by simulations, models, pure images and representations" (1998: 10). Thus, the idea of India that is produced by the hotelier is imagined and done for financial gain. Another notion that is reproduced through this picture is of the lying native that is present in Western Orientalist discourses such as of Kipling and Forster. The History House has undergone great change. It is no longer dark and evil:

> Kari Saipu's house had been renovated and painted. It had become the centrepiece of an elaborate complex. . . . The colonial bungalow . . . was surrounded by smaller, older, wooden houses—ancestral homes—that the hotel chain had bought from old families and transplanted in the Heart of Darkness. . . . The Hotel people liked to tell their guests that the oldest of the wooden houses, with its air-tight, panelled storeroom which could hold enough rice to feed an army for a year, had been the ancestral house of E.M.S. Namboodiripad, 'Kerala's Mao Tse-Tung,' they explained to the uninitiated. The furniture and knick-knacks that came with the house were on display. A reed umbrella, a wicker couch. A wooden dowry box. They were labelled with edifying placards which said *Traditional Kerala Umbrella* and *Traditional Bridal Dowry Box*. (126)

The location of the wooden houses and the bungalow is another element of othering. The colonial bungalow represents the powerful colonizers and the small wooden houses are a symbol of the peripheral Other who is not as strong and powerful as the colonizer. E.M.S. Namboodiripad's house and the items that are put on display signify exotica. The blending together of the Western and the native elements is illustrated with sarcasm: "So there it was then History and Literature enlisted by commerce. Kurtz and Karl Marx joining palms to greet rich guests as they stepped off the boat" (126). By making fun of the fusion of the local and colonial fundamentals, Roy is critical of communism as it is practised in Kerala. It is a hybrid Communism that is interested in capitalism as is depicted by the readiness of the Keralese to market the historical artefacts of their Communist leader.

The Kathakali dance is also one of the attractions of Kerala.2 It is exotic as it relates the story from the *Mahabharata*, which is indigenously Indian. In the fiction, we are told, the dancers perform at the new hotel for tourists. The performance is said to be "Truncated Kathakali performance" (127). It is only performed to give the tourists a flavour or sample of Indian culture. However, the foreign audience do not give due attention even to this edited performance.

The Kathakali dancer is rendered fascinating. We are told: "The Kathakali Man is the most beautiful of men" (230). Then we are informed that today the Kathakali dancer is not appreciated either by his family or society. He is set apart from the everyday Indian. The exoticist approach that "concentrates on the wondrous aspect of India" (28), is being employed in the description of the Kathakali man and dance.

Another example of the exoticist approach will be discussed. The approach is working when the story of the five Pandava brothers from the *Mahabharata* is told via the description of the Kathakali dance (231-36). This narration is for the benefit of the Western readers who are not familiar with the stories from the Hindu religious text. Roy is doing what Sen accuses politicians of, that is to retell the stories from the Hindu religious texts and mythology in order to extend their political agenda. While politicians do it to gain votes, the writer has done it to sell her work to the West.

The dancers are also representations of the stereotyped Other. The image of the uncivilized Indian is depicted via the Kathakali dancers. Their beauty is turned into bestiality when they go home after their performance to abuse their spouses: "The Kathakali Men took off their make-up and went home to beat their wives" (236). The beauty of the dance and dancers is portrayed using the exoticist approach and the ugliness is an echo of the Orientalist idea of the uncivilized Other. Both splendour and repulsiveness manage to Other India and its people in the eyes of the Western readers and make the country, culture and people exotic.

The God of Small Things is a fiction that adheres to the Orientalist framework that was created by the colonizers. We can see that characters, theme and plot are exoticized and presented as stereotypes in order to comply with the Western framework, that has been set since Orientalism, in the rendition of the story of the Other.

The author and publishers may deny the fact that the novel is written based on a formula of what sells in the West. However, this research shows that the fiction delivers portraits of India, of its people and of its culture that are exotic to the West, and that the West loves to see, and thus exploits them for the Western market. *The God of Small Things* does not give a new meaning to the story of India as a postcolonial nation. What it provides for its reading public is gloom—India vis-à-vis the fiction is presented as the Heart of Darkness. It grants the West with the already set notion that the East is dark and evil.

NOTES

1. This is explained by R.K. Dhawan in his paper "Arundhati Roy: The Novelist Extraordinary," R.K. Dhawan, ed., 1999. *Arundhati Roy: The Novelist Extraordinary*. New Delhi: Prestige. 11-22.
2. A detail description and explanation of the Kathakali dance and dancer can be found in T.S. Satyan "Kathakali Dramatic Dance," *Discover India*, April 1995, vol. 8, no. 4, 34-37.

Works Cited

Al Atas, S.H. 1977. *The Myth of the Lazy Native*.

Dhawan, R. K. 1999. *Arundhati Roy: The Novelist Extraordinary*. New Delhi: Prestige.

Fanon, Frantz 1977. *The Wretched of the Earth* [1961], trans. Constance Farrington, New York: Grove Press.

Fanon, Frantz. 1970. (1952). *Black Skin, White Masks*, trans. Charles Lam Markmann. St. Albans: Paladin.

Gupta, Dipankar. 2000. *Mistaken Modernity: India between Worlds*. New Delhi: HarperCollins.

Kipling, Rudyard. 1950. (1901) *Kim*.

Roy, Arundhati. 1997. *The God of Small Things*. London: Flamingo.

Roy, Arundhati. 1998. "The End of Imagination." *The Nation*. http://www.the nation.com/issue/980928/0928AROY.HTM.

Said, Edward. 1995 (1978). *Orientalism*. London: Penguin.

Said, Edward. 1994. (1993). *Culture and Imperialism*. London: Vintage.

Sardar, Ziauddin. 2000. *The Consumption of Kuala Lumpur*. London: Reaktion.

Sardar, Ziauddin. 1998. *Postmodernism and the Other: The New Imperialism of Western Culture*. London: Pluto Press.

Satyan, T.S. "Kathakali Dramatic Dance," *Discover India*. April 1995. Vol. 8, no. 4. 34-37.

Sen, Amartya. 1993. "Indian and the West: our distortions and their consequences," *The New Republic*. June 7, 1993. Vol. 208, No. 23, 27-33.

Toor, Saadia. 2000. "Indo-Chic: The Cultural Politics of Consumption in Post-Liberalization India," *SOAS Literary Review* (2). July 2000. http://www.soas.ac.uk/soaslit/ issue2/TOOR.PDF.

Note: This essay has been extracted from Halimah Ali. *Orientalism from Within: Arundhati Roy and Her Contemporaries*. Palau Pinang: Penerbit Universiti Sains Malaysia, 2011.

Journey of a Regressive Daughter for Self-Identity: Manju Kapur's *Difficult Daughters*

NILOFAR JABIN
Res. Sch., Jaipur National University, Jaipur

Modern Indian fiction has given vent to Indian feminine sensibility; their increasing awareness, strong determination to face men's hypocrisy and their search for self-fulfilment and individual identity. It gained its importance and sustenance from various social and political happenings, events that were taking place like Indian freedom movement, her independence and her quest for her own identity, right to vote, growing awareness and the spread of education, employment opportunities and legal developments for the protection of women's rights and the inner self-assertion for her position in the society equivalent to men and to be free from their suppression.

Indian literary resonance that started with the pioneering works of Raja Rao and R.K. Narayan is in full acne today, establishing dominance in Indian literature. The literary world has warmly welcomed the Indian English women writers with the greatest impact on the literary world by Arundhati Roy winning the Booker Prize for *The God of Small Things* in 1997. As a result more and more women writers are articulating and expressing their anxieties about the position of women in Indian society. The image of the woman which was depicted in the earlier novels as a passive and helpless individual has gradually been replaced with the emergence of the New Woman. Individual identity and self-assertion led to the emergence of a new woman resisting cultural oppression and to an extent being successful. Female characters in Manju Kapur's novels are some of the best representations of this phenomenon.

Manju Kapur is one of the most talked about Indian women novelists. Her works gained importance because they deal with the core problems and sufferings of women that they faced earlier and are going through the suppression of the male-dominated society. The position of woman varies from culture to culture but her position never gained equal importance in the patriarchal society.

Manju Kapur's debut novel *Difficult Daughters*, published in 1998 and winner of the Commonwealth Writer's Prize in 1999, has beautifully portrayed the core problems that women are facing in the male-dominated Indian society. She has presented a new perspective regarding the woman who is bold, compassionate and assertive. In the novel, Manju Kapur highlights the issue of patriarchy and forced gender roles which deny women the freedom to express themselves freely. Her characters are daughters who are struggling for their self-identity. The era of subjugation is gone and women have started to fight for their rights and struggle against the oppressive mechanism of a closed society. The present paper portrays a new woman who is bold and brave and capable of taking decisions independently.

Manju Kapur's *Difficult Daughters*, a captivating literary work, is her splendid contribution to Indian English novel. She beautifully lays the Indian concept in her mind and her characters are the people of the middle class. Virmati is a vivid picture of a woman who is psychologically dependent on the old patterns, norms and traditions of the society as a whole. She is born to be enslaved in the clutches of the closed patriarchal society.

The story is an intriguing tale of a mother recounted by her daughter, set at the time of partition. She belonged to a wealthy family. The novel highlights the issue of patriarchy and forced gender roles that suppresses a women's voice and her freedom. Virmati refuses to follow the set norms and restrictions of the society of that time. Her daughters are characters who do not fit into this male-dominated society and a never ending question of her self-identity continues. Her struggles continue as women did not have the liberty to choose their own life.

The novel opens with a cryptic statement: 'The one thing that I wanted was not to be like my mother.' The lines are said by Ida. It is the story of a woman who faces the turbulence of family liabilities, her intense longing for education and to be loved. The protagonist being the eldest child of Kasturi has got the duty of taking care of her ten younger brothers and sisters. Born and brought up in a traditional family her mother's priority was that she should get married to a nice boy of her parents' choice even though she herself was an educated woman. However, after completion of high school she refuses to marry and settle down. Virmati was deeply influenced by her cousin, Shakuntala, who was a M.Sc. in chemistry and works at Lahore College. She is independent, self-assured, career-oriented and believes in the idea of being something in her life. In her intimate conversation, she tells Virmati: "Here we are, fighting for the freedom of the nation, but women are still supposed to marry and nothing else" (14). She always inspires Virmati, the protagonist, to think above and to fight for other causes of life either national or social. She says: "Times are changing, and women are moving out of the house, so why not you?" (16)

Highly influenced by the ways of Shakuntala, her cousin's freedom and exposure to the outside world of travelling and interacting with people in seminars one day, she replies, 'I want to be like you, Pehnji." It was a resemblance that her inner self was struggling for--a life that she had been dreaming for herself long before her meeting with the Oxford-returned professor, Harish. This is reflected every time when the novelist is speaking about the protagonist's mind. "It was useless looking for answers inside the home. One had to look outside. To education, freedom and the bright lights of Lahore colleges." (17)

As the story proceeds, we find that Virmati was not granted the permission to pursue her further studies and she starts living in a dilemma that her future lies in her own hands. Unfortunately she fails in her F.A. exams and the chaos begins in her life when her parents start looking for a suitable boy and compel her to get married. In spite of this turbulence of life, she insists on reappearing for her F.A. exams and starts studying in the college. She was the seventh girl among four hundred boys. She takes help from the professor in her studies but cannot realize the greediness in the eyes of the professor of his need for companionship rather than help.

Further, in the last line of chapter VIII Manju Kapur remarks the following where she informs the readers how Virmati finally gets embroiled in professor's deceitful inclination of possessing her: "But by then the desire to possess her had already reached her heart and mind." (47)

She falls in love with a romantic married professor who was her neighbour. Virmati later finds that her life was in difficulty. She was caught in an illicit hopeless love, she breaks her engagement with a decent boy Inderjit, attempts suicide and finally plans for her further studies. She goes to Lahore to live alone and continue her studies. A couple of years later she goes to Nahan to work as a principal in one of the schools which is the capital of Sirmaur.

Situated in the vicinity of the Himalayan state run by an enlightened maharaja, she lives happily and considers this to be the most peaceful period of her life. Working as the headmistress of a girl's school, she is able to regulate all positive aspects in her life. Being competent in her work and all the professional skills she was given due respect which made her inner self satisfied as being an independent women with no liabilities, no one to command her and with a space of her own. She lived away from home for almost a year and declared that society would be better off if females were effective and capable enough. She would solve her problems herself. She was worthy of independence. She had a room for herself which provides her psychological and mental peace. It would have been easy for Manju Kapur to cast Virmati in the role of a victim but she does not do so. Virmati is portrayed as a strong woman in her life.

When Virmati returns as the professor's second wife, she has a deeper understanding of things by reading books and gathering information as compared to the girls of her time and the situations prevalent at that time.

Virmati's rebellion towards her very traditional Arya Samaj family that constituted of her family, grandparents, aunts and all the family that lived jointly, her postponing of the marriage and her refusal to marry the boy whom the family had selected and to whom she was engaged, constitutes a radical rebellious act, which predicts an individual, who would go to any extent to fulfil her desires and set forth a feminist statement. Her sufferings for the sake of love, and marriage to Professor Harish Chandra, who is already married to Ganga and has a child, point towards a 'self' who is strong and assertive.

Two factors that enable a modern woman to be independent and capable are education and economic independence. Virmati comes to us as a modern woman, as an individual who is educated as well as economically independent before marriage. Its reality lies in the fact that she was able to break the patriarchal mode in the 1940s is in itself a great achievement. She thus awakens in a world of self experience to acquire her complete identity and independence. Her daughter Ida, a divorced and childless woman, leads a much freer life than her mother. In fact she was able to achieve more than her mother was able to achieve. She struggles throughout to free herself from the inferiority of the females and assert the importance of a woman. She returns home and joins her mother to stay and feels that real happiness lies in the closeness of the mother. She thus appears to be in tune with herself, her wishes and to be sure not to succumb that valuable self of hers to any pressures applied externally.

Works Cited

Bala, Suman and Subhash Chandra. "Manju Kapur's *Difficult Daughters*: An Absorbing Tale of Fact and Fiction." *50 Years of Indian Writing*, ed. R.K. Dhawan. New Delhi: Indian Association for English Studies.

Barnes, Djouns. *Nightwood* (New York: New Dimensions, 1961).

Cassier, Ernest. 1994. *An Essay on Man*. New Haven, Comn: Yale University Press.

Kapur, Manju. *Difficult Daughters* (Penguin India, 1998).

Bridging the Two Nations: Jhumpa Lahiri's *The Lowland*

SUMAN BALA
S.B.S. College, University of Delhi

Diaspora Studies is one of the most important areas of critical attention in the contemporary literary circles. What exactly is Diaspora? It is a mode of cultural production that involves the production and reproduction of transnational social and cultural phenomenon. The term 'diaspora' and 'expatriate' have become mutually synonymous in the wake of the emergence of substantial literature in the field. Most of the writings veer around the experiences of the "diasporic Indian," of one whose very self-hood is defined by the primary fact of its displacement. And it is the process of the transformation that he or she undergoes which is of significance to the readers.

Indians, settled overseas, have produced a store of valuable literature that has received international recognition. Though their writings, writes P. Padmavathi in her insightful essay "Diaspora," these writers make a conscious effort to re-establish social and cultural patterns whose roots may be traced back to India and its culture. These writers—be they in America, England, Canada or Australia—share a common experience—trauma of being away from their homeland, of an imaginary homeland to which they have to return one day. The diaspora writers produce a kind of literature that probes their cultural identity in the face of an overwhelming Western identity. In the process, they produce a rich literature that is essentially multicultural, intellectual, transcultural, paving way for global literature.

Indian-American literature, though young, is making fast strides. It began with the writing of memoirs—accounts of the recollection of the homeland and personal response to the 'new' world. In this connection, Ved Mehta made a substantial contribution by his autobiographical works *Daddyji* and *Mamaji*. With Bharati Mukherjee migrating from Canada to U.S.A., diaspora literature recorded the first major change. Mukherjee's fictional world is larger, but she continues with the autobiographical tradition of Ved Mehta and many other Indo-American fiction writers.

The importance of identity has been a core area of Asian American writing. Interestingly, the identity of the Asian writer cannot be categorized in simple, neat terms—Eastern and Western. All the writers live between the push and pull of opposing cultural forces, resulting in the creation of an identity that is multiple and transnational. Prominent figures like Chitra Divakaruni and Jhumpa Lahiri have emerged as significant diaspora writers who belong to the second generation of Indian immigrants in the U.S. and deal with the conditions of young generation that is neither 'here' nor 'there.' Jhumpa Lahiri confesses this in an interview given to Rachel Hore: "I wrote about people whose very existence has been shaped by unsettlement." Similarly, Chitra Divakaruni dwells at length on the theme of identity in her writings. The sense of alienation and sickness in exile has sufficiently been explored by these writers. Chitra Divakaruni's famous novel *Queen of Dreams* portrays the picture of an immigrant woman, Rakhie, who having been born and submerged by an alien culture, fashions her own identity in order to survive and succeed in the liminal space.

The Lowland is the second novel by Lahiri. It tells us the story of two brothers who came of age in the 1960s, in the city of Calcutta. It takes inspiration from the political movement that causes an upheaval both in the country, as also in the life of the major characters in the novel. Udayan, the younger of the two brothers, gets drawn into a radical movement called Naxalism, its name derived from Naxalbari, a tiny village in the north of Calcutta. It was essentially a peasants' movement against the landlords and police in 1967. The activists in this movement were inspired by Mao's revolution in China.

The title of the novel raises some suspense. What is 'lowland': it is a scrap of vacant land in Tollygunge, Calcutta, which floods after the monsoon and fills with water hyacinth. Among the children who use it as a shortcut in the 1950s are Subhash and Udayan, a clerk's sons. Subhash, the older brother, is obedient and reserved in temperament, Udayan is independent-minded, stubborn and charismatic. Each has a gift for science. They bring up a radio and follow the news as the years go by. That is how they get to know about the Maoist-inspired uprising in Darjeeling. After the authorities crush the rebellion, shooting villagers in Naxalbari, Udayan is irresistibly drawn to the fledgling Naxalite movement. Subhash, on the other hand, concentrates on his studies. The brothers divided by their outlook, the plot of the story takes a new turn.

It is Subhash who makes the first move as he leaves for Rhode Island to do postgraduate studies in oceanography. Meanwhile, Udayan, now a teacher, informs Subhash by letter that he has got married without consulting their parents. Then a telegram arrives: "Udayan killed. Come back if you can." In Calcutta, his crushed parents won't tell him what happened, so he gets the details from his brother's widow Gauri. She was a former student, whose role in the family is to perform menial domestic duties, keeping up the Indian traditions. Subhash learns about the tragic events. Udayan had involved himself in a revolutionary violence; and during a police search, he had hid himself in the lowland, but was found out and shot in full view of the neighbourhood. Gauri, we learn, is pregnant and the parents plan to send her back to her parents while keeping the child. To rescue Gauri from this situation, Subhash marries her. In course of time, Gauri gives birth to a girl child who is named Bela.

Though Subhash is not the real father of Bela, he gives her love. While in the United States, Bela adapts herself to the American culture, having liaison with many and not leading a settled life. She gives birth to a child Meghna, but does not stick to the father of the girl. Like Lahiri's earlier fiction, there are elements of discord and alienation, hope and rejection, and love and loss. While at one time, Subhash had made a sacrifice by marrying his brother's wife in order to give her care and shelter, the marriage starts to crumble, leading to many other problems. Subhash is equally worried about his aging parents in Calcutta as they need care and support. The novelist juxtaposes the conflict between Subhash's comfortable life in the East Coast in America versus the debilitating life of his parents in Calcutta.

The cultural divide is also evident in the portrayal of the character of Gauri. Her act of rebellion for self-identity and the way she charts out her independent life in America stands out. Gauri becomes self-dependent by taking up a teaching job. It is interesting to note that while there is a physical union between Gauri and Subhash, she does not accept him as her lover. In due course, she distances herself and moves out of his life, leaving behind her daughter Bela with him. Commenting on this development, Christopher Taylor remarks in *London Review of Books* that the story takes a turn once Gauri and Subhash are there together in America: "likely avenue of development—accommodation with the past, and perhaps the flowering of love, against a backdrop of immigrant life in New England." After brooding for months, Gauri rips up her saris, shortens her long hair, and diverts herself to studies, exploring a new world in the campus. While she has given birth to a daughter, she pursues an academic career in philosophy. Her attachment with Subhash is circumstantial. It is only in the interest of her child Bela that she comes closer to him. She starts sleeping with him only keeping this in mind. By the time Bela is 12, she has grown used to her mother's absence and impatient outbursts.

Bela takes the situation in her stride. She is not surprised that Gauri does not join them on a visit to Calcutta. She does not even know that Subhash is not her biological father. Subhash is reluctant to share this with her lest she be shocked. They return to the U.S. to find a note from Gauri explaining that she would like to teach philosophy in California and wanted no further contact.

The Lowland has taken the literary world by storm. It has great academic value. The unquestioned contrast in personalities of the two central brothers has a mythological quality. Unlike Lahiri's earlier works, it is layered and complex. The plot and story have so many intricacies that it is fascinating experience to unravel them. It is a beautiful piece of fiction that needs to be read: the novel is really about people anywhere facing life's challenges and how they respond.

A critical evaluation of Jhumpa Lahiri's latest work *The Lowland* reinforces the fact that Indian writers of the second generation are making a substantial contribution to the mainstream contemporary American literature. Especially works by women writers—Indira Ganesan's *The Journey*, Chitra Divakaruni's *The Mistress of Spices*, Amulya Malladi's *The Mango Season*, Kiran Desai's *The Inheritance of Loss*. All these writers have the settings of their novels either in India or in the West but they are successful in bridging the gap between two nations/ cultures and in the process give rise to transnational literature which has a global import.

Assertion of the Female Subaltern Voice in Bama's Fiction

R.K. DHAWAN
S.B.S. College, University of Delhi
SUMITA PURI
Dyal Singh (E) College, University of Delhi

In the mid-20th century, the term 'subaltern' began to be used as a reference to the colonized people in the South-African subcontinent. In the early 1980s, the term gained a momentum, when at Oxford, Subaltern Studies Group (SSG) was formed under the leadership of Ranajit Guha. It was a group of South Asian scholars, who were interested in the postcolonial and post-imperial societies in South Asia in particular and the developing world in general. In the recent decades, it is regularly used as a term in history, anthropology, sociology and literature.

Historically and politically, subaltern literature is the outcome of European Imperialism. It was mostly in the 19th century when European countries, especially Britain, tried consolidating the imperial power. In the garb of development, Europeans exploited the natives and indigenous people of occupied lands. The process involved military conflict, the massive displacement of the people and greed for profit. But more than accumulation of wealth, it entailed ideological notions of 'subject races,' 'subordinate people and justified the necessity of imposing authority on those, seen as inferior. This was a period in which economic supremacy and political authority of Europe became global.

By 1815, Britain had established itself as a dominant power in the world, as the leader of industrialization and expansion. The time of Queen Victoria's reign, from 1837 to 1901, represented the great age of colonization. It was a time, when there was a wide expansion of the British Empire and the spreading of imperial ideas. Britain, it was believed, had a duty and destiny to rule the world. They were backed by industrial and military power. A special feature of this ideology, was their strong belief, that European science, politics and religion were superior to any other. Hence emerged the belief, that reality should be interpreted in these terms.

Along with the belief in Eurocentrism, they also believed that colonized people were lesser human beings—less human, less civilized, and less cultured, more like savages. European anthropologists considered colonized people as primitive, barbarian, inferior, unfit to rule or manage their resources. So, it was the Whiteman's burden to civilize and educate them.

Subaltern literature, thus, articulates the unsaid and unheard ordeal of the marginalized. Unlike Dalit men, only a few Dalit women have written their personal narratives that still remain nameless and faceless in the so-called mainstream literary circles. A major handicap for Dalit women is their lack of education and the ensuing inability to pen down their experiences. The number of literate among Dalits is abysmally low. Majority of these women lead simple and ordinary lives, busy earning their livelihood. They work very hard to survive, as they are much below the poverty line. Despite these challenges, some Dalit women have been able to narrate their sorrows and pains.

It is mainly education and ushering of democracy that brought slow transformation in society. It awakened all sections of society—Dalits, Adivasis and nomadic tribes were no exception. The period from 1920 to 1956 was vastly influenced by Dr. B.R. Ambedkar. This period is often called the Renaissance phase in the history of the Dalit movement. Ambedkar founded

Siddhartha College in Mumbai in 1946 and Milind College in Aurangabad in 1947. These colleges acted as catalysts that promoted the young generation to express their sentiments in writing. The Dalits consolidated themselves and held the first conference of Dalit writers in the auditorium of Bengali High School, Dadar, on 2 March 1958. At this conference, a resolution was passed to announce the entry of Dalit literature as a perfect segment of knowledge. Further, it was argued that only Dalits had the experience and authority to narrate the pain of Dalits.

Further, it was argued that only Dalits had the experience and authority to narrate the pain of Dalits. Though Mulk Raj Anand has been generally hailed as the writer of the suffering humanity and a strong advocate of the cause of the poor, yet he was not accepted by Dalits as their representative, because he belonged to a higher caste. Personal experience was said to be the basis of Dalit writing.

Dalit literature has many affinities with African-American literature. Both these literatures are the outcome of movements for human right and against exploitation. The most popular form of writing for Dalit and other subaltern writers is the autobiography. Expression of self is the most important feature of a work of art. Autobiography is the mirror in which the writer reflects his own image. However, man's image in the mirror is visible, not only to himself, but also to the people around him. This is what establishes the relationship between self and society.

Alice Walker is one of the most admired African American feminist writers. She is best known for her novel *The Color Purple*, published in 1982. It is an epistolary novel, made up of letters written by Celie. Celie is s fourteen-year-old vulnerable girl, who addresses her letters to 'Dear God.' She has three children by her father. She fights her way to life and questions everything she has been taught. Living in Chicago, Celie spreads her wings. She opens up her own tailor shop and learns to make pants both for women and men. Although the novel is mainly about Celie and her life, it highlights the journeys of the other women, who are in her life, including Shug, Nettie, and Sophia. Together, these women help one another to discover beauty and identity in themselves. Feeling inspired by each other, they muster strength to overcome their oppressive men and emancipate themselves from their clutches. Like Alice Walker, Bama too exhorts the underprivileged women to fight back and not accept humiliation lying down.

Like Bama, Aboriginal writers too have been fighting for their rights. *My Place* is an autobiography written by Australian author Sally Morgan. Written in 1987, it is about Morgan's quest for knowledge of her own family's past. The story relates to a young girl growing up to false heritage and not knowing where she is from. The narrative revolves around Morgan's own hometown Perth, Western Australia. Morgan travels to her grandmother's birthplace, exploring a search for her family. She discovers her indigenous Australian heritage—information that was kept secret so far because of the social stigma. Morgan is an Aboriginal ambassador who wants indigenous Australia to feel pride in their identity rather than shame. Like Morgan, Dalit feminist Bama, has in her novels, attempted to articulate and record her experiences of hurt, humiliation and historical neglect by the elite over centuries.

Using the "discourse of participation," and drawing from a narrative that speaks about ordinary lives, the Dalit texts convey the voices of women who are on the margins in society. In this context, the most significant name that comes to our mind is that of Bama.

Faustina Mary Fatima Rani, also known as Bama Faustina Soosairaj is a Tamil Dalit feminist writer who was born in 1958 in a Roman Catholic family in Pudhupatti, Madras, and a small village in South Tamil Nadu. She belongs to a family of Dalits who had been agricultural labourers and had converted to Christianity. She completed the eighth standard in the village school.

While she was in her village, she experienced discrimination based on caste, class and gender. The desire to transgress takes us back to her childhood memory of playing kabaddi with her four siblings. She admits, "Sometimes we were cops and robbers, sometimes husband and wife. But my favourite game was kabaddi (a team wresting game played in many Indian villages). I liked the whole business of challenging, crossing over and vanquishing the opponent."[1]

During school holidays, she used to accompany her grandfather to work in the Naicker landlord's fields. She had seen how her grandfather and grandmother were ill-treated, because of their caste and status. The other force that propelled her to liberate her from the fetters of hegemonic relations was her father's insistence on education. A voracious reader, Bama read Tamil writers like Jayakantan, Mani, Parthasarathy and Rabindranath Tagore, to name a few. These influences had a telling effect on the young Bama. She, thus, emerged as a significant voice in Dalit women's writing, not just because of the forceful portrayal of atrocities on Dalits, but also because the very act of writing becomes an act of empowerment.

Despite the misery in early life, Bama had a carefree childhood and her brother Raj Gauthaman, also a writer, introduced her to the world of books and inspired her to write poetry. Later, she turned to writing fiction. After acquiring college education, Bama became a school teacher. In her writings, she depicts the oppression she faced as a student and as a teacher. Her life took a big turn when at the age of 26, she took a vow to become a nun. But even in the convent, she realized that the situation for Dalits was no better. Thus, seven years later, in 1992, Bama walked out of convent, and decided to write her experiences in the form of biography, that saved her from ending her life in the midst of all the struggles. The resultant work *Karukku* was hailed as a masterpiece and Bama shot to prominence in literary circles. Literature enabled her to empower herself and to empower others as well. She created her pen name Bama which stands for a blend of sounds. Bama is the pen name of Faustina Mary Fatima Rani. In Tamil, Fatima is pronounced as Batima, and from that came 'Bama.'

Hailed as the first Dalit woman writer in India, Bama's *Karukku* is the first autobiography of its kind in Tamil Dalit literature. The autobiography received the anticipated criticism leading to her banishment from her village for the next seven months. The work, however, received critical acclaim and was awarded the Crossword Book Award in 2000. Bama became a recognized name and published more works thereafter to fundamentally challenge and overthrow hierarchies and to re-search the Dalit female identity. Her publications include her autobiography, *Karukku* (1992), which has been translated into English, two novels, *Sangati* (1994) and *Vanmam* (2002), and three collections of short stories, *Kisumbukkaran* (1996), *Oru Thathavan Oru Erumayum* (2003) and *Kondattam* (2009). *Sangati* and *Kisumbukkaran* have been translated into French.

Bama's fiction pronounces her as a leader of the downtrodden and a harbinger of social change. Her works communicate her voice in support of Dalits, referred to as 'taazhttapatoor' or 'odukkapattor' in Tamil, meaning 'marginalized' or 'oppressed.' The word 'taazhapattor' was used by Bharati Dasan in his poem "Taazhtapattor samattuvapaattu" or "Song for the equality of the oppressed."[2] In her words, "I use writing as one of the weapons to fight for the rights of the underprivileged."[3] When Bama left the convent and her village with a sense of alienation, *Karukku* was born. The painful moments of having lived a life of a doubly marginalized—a Dalit and then a woman—inspired her to express this suffocation and anguish. *Karukku* does not belong to the conventional formalized archetype of the autobiography. The first of its kind in Tamil language, the work does not follow a linear pattern of events. The protagonist is unnamed and many episodes are presented through various viewpoints. Instead of reflecting upon her life's journey, the writer chooses to interpret the narrative from a larger perspective—her pain signifying the pain of her community. From the childhood memoirs of discrimination between the sexes to the comparative analysis of Dalit culture and the elitist institution of the church, *Karukku* makes the text, a study in Dalit literature in general.

Following this, Bama published *Sangati*, in 2005. The work witnesses a shift from the personal to the general. While *Karukku* is an autobiography of an individual, *Sangati* is the autobiography of a community. *Sangati*, as the title signifies, is composed of events. It offers a series of stories of real life, narrated by different women characters. These stories are accompanied by general comments and author's opinions. *Sangati* records the lives of Dalit women, who face double oppression—from the upper caste as also from patriarchy, male authority.

Sangati does not follow the parameters of a traditional novel. It has no plot in the normal sense; it has many stories told by different protagonists. Sangati means news, events, happenings and the book, therefore, has interconnected anecdotes. Bama makes it clear in her Acknowledgement to the volume:

> My mind is crowded with many anecdotes: stories not only about the sorrows and tears of Dalit women, but also about their lively and rebellious nature.

Sangati is a manifesto for equality and emancipation of women. It tells us about the double standards of men: they get better wages than women for working in the fields and in the construction work. Women are also vulnerable to sexual harassment and abuse in the work market. Apart from economic disparity, they are maltreated at home by fathers, husbands and brothers.

Sangati deals with several generations of women: the older women, like the narrator's grandmother Vellaiamma, writer—her own self and the generation coming after her. The book is in the voices of many women speaking and addressing one another as they share the incidents of their daily lives. There is a special quality of these women. They may be oppressed and tortured, but they do not take things lying down. They are not simplistic; they are subtle women. They have the ability of undermining the authority figures by ridiculing them, or playing tricks on them. They may be suffering, but nonetheless they can laugh at their masters.

Sangati became extremely popular with the readers because of the message it gave. It is the message of self-confidence instead of self-pity. You can acquire this confidence if you are educated. Women in *Sangati* do not lack confidence; rather they make fun of them who oppressed them. They have the courage to revolt. In Author's Note, Bama says: "These women swim against the tide and have self-respect and vitality." The stories in the book are based on memories of personal experience of Dalit women, narrated in first person.

Women in *Sangati* go through the process of metamorphoses. It is a passage from innocence to experience. In the earlier stories, we get a graphic picture of Dalit women—as infants, young girls, who are oppressed, mal-treated, persecuted. We are told how girls suffer hardships in the villages. There was indeed a great disparity between the two sexes. Birth of a girl was not welcome. Girls were given shabby treatment—they would not go to school; they would do domestic chores and stay confined to home. On the other hand, boys got preferential treatment and were free to indulge in frivolous activities.

In the latter part of the book, we have stories where women, though still suffering, have the courage to face the world. A typical story of the emerging bold woman is the story number Six. It is a story of the disharmony between a husband and his wife—Pakkiaraj and Raakkamma. The couple has frequent quarrels. Most interesting is the scene between the husband and his wife facing each other in a fight in the street. We find that the husband is abusing his wife, Raakkamma, in a vulgar manner. He was hitting her body and hurling filthy abuses. If he was showering abuses, she was equally giving it back:

> "You are a vile creature. You can take on a woman. Bastard, go and fight with a man who is your equal. You will be taught a lesson," and holding him in contempt, she spat at him.

This kind of retaliation by a female aimed at setting a new trend in man-woman relation in Indian society. The keynote is woman's revolt against man's oppression.

Vanmam is the third novel that envisages the subaltern dream of equity and justice in society. Set in a village called Kandampatti in Tamil Nadu, *Vanman* meaning vendetta, exposes the internal fissures in the sub communities of Parayas and Pallars and their harrowing experiences. The village streets marked for segregated castes and sub castes of Dalits and the landlords epitomizes the Indian situation in general. The personal vendetta coupled with starvation, atrocities and unreasonable quarrels within communities, leads the Dalit youth to choose the path of education and solidarity, which alone, can turn the cherished Dalit dream into reality. 'Educate! Organize! Agitate!' is the slogan which the Dalit shout to claim their individuality. The authorial voice sums it all:

> We must realize how society has marginalized us, discriminated us . . . we shall strive together to see that justice prevails. . . . Arise and face the new dawn. Don't remain docile. You have been born to rule, to live like human beings . . . we will make a new world.[4]

Bama is not pessimistic about the future of women. She asserts that women can tide over oppression and neglect if they are willing to learn and attain knowledge of the world around. In this respect, she echoes what Ambedkar had said once. Addressing women of the depressed class in 1927, Ambedkar made a significant statement which is true even today:

> You should devote yourself to learning and cultivation of the mind. Do not be in a hurry to marry. Marriage is a liability. You should

> not impose it upon your children unless they are able to meet the liabilities arising out of marriage. Above all, let every girl who marries stand by her husband but refuse to be his slave.

This is possible when a woman can make a choice between right and wrong. It can be through awareness and education. Aurobindo said that the progress or culture of a nation can be measured by the degree of progress women have made. Women are the true ambassadors of a nation's culture. A nation that neglects its culture will lose its soul and perish.

II

"A word after a word after word is power," said Margaret Atwood and Bama is an emphatic voice who has put her feminist and revolutionary ideology into praxis. Apart from imparting education to girls at a primary school in Uthiramerur near Chennai, Bama galvanizes young Dalit women 'to strive, to seek, to find, and not to yield.' Her revolt against patriarchy is also manifested in her decision to stay single and work towards the 'annihilation of caste,' fulfilling Dr. B.R. Ambedkar's vision of a casteless society. Through her powerful writing, she has incessantly worked towards the liberation of her people from the clutches of the hegemonic reckoning that shrinks Dalits to a non-entity.

The socio-cultural and religious coercive forces in the Indian context have persuaded the marginalized voices to produce literature of resistance. The struggle initiated by B.R. Ambedkar, Jyotiba Phule and Namdeo Dhasal and strengthened by Baburao Bagul, Om Prakash Valmiki, Kancha Ilaiah and Faustina Bama, has led to the institutionalization of Dalit literature and its incorporation in the canon. These writers have succeeded in the portrayal of the lived reality from an insider's perspective. They not only face the politics of resistance from the centre to remain at the fringes but also the politics of assertion from the margins to shift from their defined peripheral space. Thus, "Dalit" meaning 'crushed,' 'ground' or 'broken to pieces' faces the challenge of writing as a political act of emancipation of the Dalit self and the community as a whole. As Raj Kumar has put it, "the Dalits are trying to write themselves into the Indian narrative."[5]

The journey becomes even more demanding, when a Dalit woman decides to raise her voice. Her task is to overthrow the dominant ideologies and societal structures and embolden the oppressed sex. Faustina Bama, thus, chooses a non-conformist style in her autobiography as well as novels to protest against the codified stereotypes of class, caste and gender. Her works provide a nuanced and panoramic view of Dalit life. At the same time, she hopes that the suppression of her people leads to upliftment through education. To conclude, Bama proves that despite the ideological positions endorsed by the dominant sex, class, caste and religion, the 'subaltern can and should speak!'

NOTES

1. nirupamad.blogspot.in/2008/10/writer-called-bama.html
2. www.outlookindia.com/website/story/introduction-to-karukku/211413
3. www.thehindu.com/thehindu/mp/2003/03/06/stories/2003030600570300.htm
4. Bama. *Vanman*, trans. Malini Seshadri. New Delhi: OUP, 2008, p. 61.
5. http://timesofindia.indiatimes.com/home/sunday-times/deep-focus/Dalit-literature-goes-global/articleshow/46810541.cms

Bama's *Sangati*: The Chronicles of Exploitation and Suppression of Dalit Women

C. CHANNAPPA
SMR First Grade College, Shankaraghatta

'Art is an important weapon in the struggle, it either reinforces or undermines the powers of oppressor' (Ngugi wa Thiong'o)

Bama (1958), in her life as well as in her writings, fearlessly advocates and nudges the cause of the downtrodden and the underprivileged particularly, the anguish of Dalit women. For historical reasons the world was divided on two major concepts—one on 'capitalism and another on 'socialism.' The interesting fact is that apart from these two divisions of the world, whatever was left over nations was called 'third world.'

Even at the time of a rapid assimilation of western cultures and non-western cultures which have been at the forefront, the marginalized sections of Indian society, still struggle to establish their existence and identity even after six decades of Independence. Feminism and Dalit feminism may not necessarily be looked differently as both have some common features. The present work in question—*Sangati* (Events) may be studied, keeping in mind 'the feminist movement, the Dalit movement, and the tribal movement led by the Naxalites.' (Bahl)

Bama's question is why do Dalit women demand the opportunity to live with respect, with social status even now? Indian situation is that the upper-caste-rich people are not ready to sacrifice their traditionally built hegemonic identity and at the same time the untouchable-marginalized Dalit women identity. The conflicts between these two extreme categories of upper caste and lower caste have been demonstrated time and again. Radhika makes a note on identity: 'Identity crisis as a problem has gained currency in this era. Usually it happens in two contexts: a person may have more than one identity and he has to arrive at a dominant one. Or else, he may not have any identities at all. In any of these situations one has to find an identity of his/her own. The fact is that a person cannot live without an identity, which makes him get recognized in the world. Why do we have a problem called identity crisis? What are the circumstances that lead to such a problem?'[1]

To substantiate the foregrounding saga of Bama's society, it would be good to know some of the male writers who write about the man-woman relationship which is always broken, rotten and tragic. For example, U.R. Ananthamurthy, a renowned Kannada writer in his ever debated novel *Samskara,* portrays the inner urge of sexual desire of Praneshachari, an orthodox Brahmin, towards an oppressed woman, Leo Tolstoy's *Anna Karenina* where Anna who is bewitching, but because of her inner sexual desire towards man, is tragically killed. A Kannada feminist writer, Vaidehi, in her a very powerful short story "Sougandhi's Soliloquies" depicts the inner dilemmas of Sougandhi—her problem of selection and her father's concern about her. She puts a number of questions about the man-woman relationship. The women writers seem to write differently from time to time. The present day women writers are aggressive, challenging, with a voice of protest and demanding equal rights.

Historically speaking women have been given lesser importance and women have been treated as giving comforts, kindness and love, though power sharing between man and woman has been debated. But Bama raises the deeper issues of Dalit women; they are treated so badly, even their fellow upper caste women too face the rigid discrimination between male and female. Sangeeta Das presents the need of the harmonious relationship between man and woman: 'Man and woman are integral parts of a society. Amiability and compatibility between the two is strident for the healthy burgeoning of the society. Man without woman and *vice-versa* cannot exist and flourish ever. Mentally both are equal though physically, man is stronger than woman no doubt but this does not endow him with the power to exploit woman. They should accept a woman as an inseparable companion and not a liability. History is evident that women have excelled not only beauty and elegance but also in brains and the egoist men have tried to curb their progress and advancement by either exerting their physical power or by incarcerating them within four walls of their houses.'"[3]

Kamala Markandaya, Nayantara Sahgal, Shashi Deshpande, Arundhati Roy, Anita Desai, Shobha De and many other novelists have written about on formally addressed urban middle class in most of the cases. These writers have used elite style of writing with attractive narration which would attract the readers. But when we talk of Dalit women writers or subaltern writers, we mean the saga of working class.

To empower the women and make them free from exploitation Marxists advocate that economic inequality should be changed completely. Then only one can find a society which is free from injustice. 'Workers and oppressed peoples of the world unite' is the Marxist slogan, which certainly advocates all the exploited class should be united to make life meaningful. Regarding Marxist views on feminism it is noted as 'Marxist feminism is a dub-type of feminist theory which focuses on the dismantling of capitalism as a way to liberate women. Marxist feminism states that private property which gives economic inequality, dependence, political confusion and ultimately unhealthy social relations between men and women, is the root of women's oppression.'[4]

Reading any translation work is not the correct way to comprehend the writer's motif. In fact, any creative art form is beyond one's capacity of understanding as Jacques Derrida confirms that the meaning of the work either 'differs' or 'defers,' even as Ngugi Wa Thiong'o, a Kenyan writer asserts 'Language carries culture and culture carries (particularly through orature and literature) the entire body of values by which we perceive ourselves and our place in the world. Therefore, how can the African experience be expressed properly in another language?' But non-Tamil speaking readers should complement Lakshmi Holmstrom for her excellent translation, even taking much care for minute psychological ad personal details. However, Bama's mute suffering can be understood in Bama's mother tongue Tamil. Channappa comments on the meaning in his book '*Indian and African Literature:* 'Literature is not mere combination of words. It is beyond the physical appearance. It is metaphysical, transcendental and cosmic. It deals with the intentions, tensions, feelings and emotions of the author. Naturally, feelings of one person may not be the feelings of another man, even in the general sense. But once, we come to specialized art called 'literature,' it is impossible to translate the same theme of the original author to the translated language. Literature is one of the finest forms which cannot be digested fully.'[5]

Autobiography is nothing but the revelations of his involvement with social tensions, and beyond all it exposes the self of the writer. But still, autobiographies may not just reflect the self but they also show the practice of social evils as Bama writes. *Sangati* is not just about Bama's individual feelings, but the writer promptly speaks on behalf of the community to which she belongs -the Dalit community. Ammalu Kutty records her observations about the necessity of writing autobiography: 'Of the ambiguities encountered in reading autobiographies, perhaps the most challenging is the question regarding the nature of self the writer reveals. The writer expounds what is prevalently called an 'identity,' a psycho-social construct made up of such elements as physical being, intellect and emotion, experience, behaviour and attitudes. The idea that the individual possesses a single fully defined 'true' self; to be either disclosed or discovered is a myth. Time and again, the complexity and contradictions of the experiences in one's life surface before us. The act of reflection may bring a new awareness of one's self, and the hard thinking about one's experience, that is an essential part of autobiography, is likely to produce new insights as to what one's self positively is. If a writer should continue this process of self-examination longer or more intensely or at a different time, or under different circumstances, the perception and presentation of the self might well be affected.'[7]

Bama's portrayal of the Dalit society reminds me of the following situation if we keep the unexplainable suffering of down-trodden in the name of purification of caste, creed and colour, as backdrop. It would be so appropriate to use a poisonous tree as a metaphor. Since the tree itself is poisonous, it cannot breed/ produce sweet fruit; similarly the Hindu society itself has the strong poisonous root which always breeds yet another poisonous fruit. The same situation can be used to human beings. Just think, centuries have passed, even after, we human beings have claimed, that we are civilized, cultured, social living being etc., though, it is also true that many sacred souls of India, such as Buddha, Basvanna, Ambedkar, Vivekananda, Mahatma Gandhi and others tried hard to cut down the branches of the poisonous tree but unfortunately as many new branches cut, the growth of the tree is becoming double the size of its original. The reason is that the roots of the tree are so deep and wide, it is rather impossible to destroy the tree as the roots have gone deeper. But still do we have the answers to the questions asked by Bama in her *Sangati* and *Karukku*?

Bama herself makes it very clear about the purpose of writing about Dalit women, 'Oppressed, ruled, and still being ruled by patriarchy, government, caste, and religion, Dalit women are forced to break all the strictures of society to live. In *Sangati,* many strong Dalit women who had the courage to break the shackles of authority, to propel themselves upwards, to roar, (their defiance) changed their difficult, problem-filled lives and quickly stanched their tears. *Sangati* is a look at part of the lives of those Dalit women who dared to make fun of the class in power that oppressed them. And through this, they found the courage to revolt.' (*Sangati*, Preface)

Lakshmi Holmstrom, who has translated *Sangati* from Tamil into English, traces the origin and need of Dalit writing. The translator of this creative work poses a very serious question, who are Dalits? Dr. B.R. Ambedkar also tried hard to define the term 'Dalit, and Mahatma Gandhi called oppressed as 'Harijans.' What we understand by the term Dalit is that the community which has been intentionally, and for political, religious reasons kept in the darker side of the society. The words of Lakshmi Holmstrom are apt and need to be mentioned here: 'The word 'Dalit' coming from Marathi and meaning 'oppressed' or 'ground down,' is not without problems in Tamil Nadu, but it has been appropriated for particular reasons: it does away with reference to caste, and points to a different kind of nation-wide constituency; specifically it signals the militancy of the Dalit Panthers, their broad definition of 'Dalit,' and their professed hope of solidarity with all oppressed groups. ('Who are Dalits? All Scheduled Castes and Scheduled Tribes, neo-Buddhists, labourers, landless and destitute peasants, women, and all those who have been exploited politically and economically and in the name of religion are Dalits.'[8]

Sangati portrays the ugly side of different people of upper castes-Dalits and even the Christian community: how do these people always exploit the helpless Dalit women. The translator has made her opinions clear by saying *Sangati* is not a novel or autobiography of individual but it speaks of invisible agony of the Dalit women community predominantly: '*Sangati,* published in Tamil in 1994, is the second work of Bama, whose earlier work, an autobiography, *Karukku,* is now well known. The tension throughout *Karukku* is between the self and the community: the narrator leaves one community (of religious women) in order to join another (as Dalit woman). *Sangati* moves from the story of individual struggle to the perception of a community of *paraiya* women, a neighbourhood group of friends and relations and their joint struggle. In this sense, *Sangati is* perhaps the autobiography of a community.' (xv)

Sangati, in simple terms, does not have well-placed artful incidents connected with a well-planned plot, though one of the prominent characters works as the narrator but still not so. The reason may be the Dalit won't have a life of sequential order. For that matter, nothing is in the order for Dalits. Naturally the judgment made by Lakshmi Holmstrom is acceptable. Regarding *Sangati,* she says: '*Sangati* flouts received notions of what a novel should be, just as *Karukku* flouts the conventions of autobiography. It has not plot in the normal sense, only the powerful stories of a series of memorable protagonists. 'Sangati' means news, events, happenings, and the book is one of interconnected anecdotes.' (xvi)

The intricacies of the language Bama uses in both *Karukku* and *Sangati,* is almost same, but *Karukku* is the voice of the single narrator whereas *Sangati* is the voices of many women, expressing their deep agony. Hence, the language is as suitable to the particular character of a group. It is artistic in its own way. 'In *Sangati,* though, Bama has made a further linguistic leap in reclaiming the language particular to the women of her community. If *Karukku* is told in Bama's own speaking voice, *Sangati* is in the voices of many women speaking to and addressing one another as they share the incidents of their daily lives.' (xix)

Bama's writing in this sense is more life oriented rather artistic, 'art for art sake' but it is more than that. As the translator speaks: 'Dalit writing has tended to consist of testimonies rather than works of imagination, chronicles rather than artistically conceived texts, lived experiences rather than poetic experimentation, and finally, a call for action rather than poetic experimentation, and finally, call for action rather than the conversion of life into art. Gross and Kannan work from a polarization of 'life' and 'art' and from value judgments based on certain assumptions about what literature should be.' (xxi)

Here one learns of Bama's ancestors joining Christianity. It is not clear whether they were forced or they voluntarily converted to Christianity. She admits the same: 'When my mother and Perimma were little children, the Christian priests came to our village. When they promised that if our people joined their faith, their children would get a free education, it seems that all the paraiyas became Christians. None of the other communities, *pallar, karavar, or chakkiliyar* did so. All of them remained Hindus. Why on earth paraiyas alone became Christians, I don't know, but because they did so at that time; now it works out that they get no concessions from the government whatsoever.' (5)

Bama is not comfortable treating boys and girls with different yard sticks and it is also true that the Dalit women are being exploited since they are in the womb. She argues and questions the discrimination: 'If a boy baby cries, he is instantly picked up and given milk. It is not so with the girls. Even with breast-feeding, it is the same story; a boy is breast-fed longer. With girls, they wean them quickly, making them forget the breast. If the boys catch an illness or a fever, they will run around and nurse them with the greatest care. If it's a girl, they'll do it half-heartedly.' (7)

Male means everything. Woman means nothing. Is this the feature of a civilized society? Bama narrates how consciously the society discriminated between male and female: 'My Paatti too was no exception in all this. She cared for her grandsons much more than she cared for us. If she brought anything home when she returned from work, it was always the grandsons she called first. If she brought cucumbers, she scooped out all the seeds with her fingernails, since she had no teeth, and gave them the remaining fruit. If she brought mangoes, we only got the skin, the stones and such; she gave the best pieces of the fruit to the boys. Because we had no other way out, we picked up and ate the leftover skins.' (8)

Bama questions the colour conflicts of white British and non-white Hindus. Bama criticizes the role of Christianity. She comments on the attitude of the white people towards their colour. Particularly the white nuns as 'That's not what I'm talking about, di. What I'm saying is, it's not just the nuns who look like that. Even the pigs they keep there are as white as anything. You get such a surprise when you see them.' (13) Bama speaks the tragic story of the villagers as Paatti narrates:

> Paatti said, 'This remind me of a young fellow, just two weeks married, who was working on a well. He was blown up when they were laying the dynamite, and died, poor man. Then there was the other man who was lifting water from a well with a leather bucket, when the bullocks went mad, dragged him round and pushed him in. He was beaten about the face and head, and he too died,' 'Even last year, a couple of kinds-both of them young girls-were helping to sow the fields with gram. They ate some of the gram, became violently sick, and then died.' (18)

Bama continues her anger about the practice of discrimination between men and women as,

> 'Whether it is right or wrong, it is better for women not to open their mouths. You try speaking out about what you believe is right. You'll only get kicked and beaten and trampled on for your pains.

> And it isn't just here that it happens, you know. It's the same throughout the world. Women are not given that kind of respect.' Paatti scrapped up the betel leaves and nut that she had crushed in her mortar, popped the mixture into her mouth, gave it a couple of good chomps, and stowed it away inside her cheek.' (29)

Sometimes, reading this novel-cum-autobiography of the society in which Bama lives is really painful and emotional and shows our helplessness as she narrates: 'I'm not talking about Kanji. Why can't we be the same as boys? *We aren't allowed to talk loudly or laugh noisily; even when we sleep we can't stretch our backs nor lie face down on our bellies. We always have to walk with our heads bowed down, gazing at our toes. You tell us all this rubbish and keep us under your control. Even when our stomachs are screaming with hunger, we mustn't eat first. We are allowed to eat only after the men in the family have finished and gone. What, Paatti, aren't we also human beings?'* (29, emphasis mine)

The Hindu society which gives more importance to boys and less importance to girls, as Bama describes the unbearable treatment between the two as she writes:

> 'It's like this from the moment we are born. One day, a number of us were sitting down to a dice-game. In the midst of this, Muukkamma from East Street turned up. 'Ei, sister-in-law Lourdu, haven't you got any common sense at all? There's your son screeching like a crow, having pissed all over the cradle-cloth. And here you are, chucking a dice around. If it were a girl at least, you could leave her to cry. But how can you come away, leaving your son bawling by himself?' . . . So you can't leave a boy baby to cry, but you can leave a girl to scream on her own, can you?' (31)

Bama questions the fateful position of women and even the darker face of the Church. She is neither happy with the Hindu way of life nor with Christianity, as she argues,

> The position of women is both pitiful and humiliating, really. In the fields they have to escape from upper-caste men's

> molestations. At church they must lick the priest's shoes and be his slaves while he threatens them with tales of God, Heaven, and Hell. Even when they go to their own homes, before they have had a chance to cook some kanji or lie down and rest a little, they have to submit themselves to their husbands' torment. (35)

Bama makes it an interesting argument about adoption of sterilization and how it is used in dual sense, as for women it is good and for men it is not good. And the writer shows how food like rice is the symbol of richness and wealth as she writes, 'If you cook it with rice, the rice grains get in the way and you never feel as if you swallowed your kuuzh. Just try the ragi-kuuzh on its own. It will slip your throat as easy as anything, with each gulp. And if you take some bites of the vegetable pickles from the Nadar's shop, in between mouthfuls, it will surely be as good as nectar from heaven.' (37)

The writer's words reflect the rigid discriminatory system of man-woman relationship. Women have been treated as subservient and their personality, their feelings and even self-respect purely depend on the judgment of the men. She narrates: 'The integrity and self-respect of the women is always based on the men's judgment that has been implemented as per social norms, tragically even woman does not indulge in adultery or affairs but still listen the words of the author, 'But Samudrakani only became furious at Patti's words. If she had only behaved herself, who would have said anything? Is there smoke without fire? Who's going to marry her now that she's lost her reputation? We should marry her off to that boy Manikkam, without any more fuss. There's no other way.' (41)

It is really too painful to read and comprehend the reality of life 'Once you've put your head in the mortar, can you escape from the pestle? No, she must continue to suffer until her head rests on the earth at last.' When my mother said this, a variety of emotions grew in my heart: anger, excitement, fury, pride, resentment, hatred.'(45)

Bama is so angry with the attitude of husbands, who never bother about their wives and their health. One can notice her concern about the well-being of the Dalit women. Don't the Dalit women have the right to question the inhuman treatment meted out to them? She writes:

> 'Night after night they must give in to their husbands' pleasure. Even it a woman's body is wracked with pain, the husband is bothered only with his own satisfaction. Women are overwhelmed and crushed by their own disgust, boredom, and exhaustion, because of all this. The stronger ones somehow manage to survive all this. The ones who don't have the mental strength are totally oppressed; they succumb to mental ill-health and act as if they are possessed by peys.' (59)

Bama's narration of Dalit women's fateful life from childhood is highly fascinating and the readers should control their breath while reading the hard reality of life: 'In our streets the girls hardly ever enjoy a period of childhood. Before they can sprout tree tender leaves, so to speak, they are required to behave like young women, looking after the housework, taking care of babies, going out to work for daily wages. Yet, in spite of all their suffering and pain one cannot but be delighted by their sparkling words, their firm tread, and their bubbling laughter.' (75)

Bama counts the reasons for men marrying the second time and the suffering of women, 'She was given away in marriage in the usual way, and she even had two children. The husband was always drunk. He couldn't give her as much as a paisa for the household expenses. On top of that, he beat her up and snatched away all that she earned. How long was she to starve? Even if she were to put up with it, what about her little children? Worse still, the ugly fellow also had another woman. Not one of Pecchi's things was safe in her own house. On top of all this, he pretty nearly killed her with his blows. The girl put up with it as long as she could, and at last went back to her father's house. . . . . 'So did she just stay there, and then get married again?' (92)

Bama does not feel shy while speaking of conversion from Hinduism to Christianity and even the conversion does not make much sense as Christianity preaches one practises another. She observes, 'My mother commented, 'If you look at it like that, it seems that it was a mistake that we ever became Christians. My Thaatha and Paatti were both Hindus. It was my mother who went and changed her name from Vellaiamma to Mariamma and converted to Christianity.' (97)

Chapter Ten, which is almost the end of the novel, describes the very interesting elements of election and voting. Bama intends to show here that how the illiterate poor people, particularly women would not understand the meaning of election and the general opinions of common people about the different political parties: 'At this point, a young fellow, Kannan, who was sitting there listening to all this, butted in. 'It must be true that women are ignorant sluts. Whoever said that there is not God? That's all nonsense. What communists say is that people shouldn't go around calling God, God, and at the same time exploiting and oppressing the working classes and labourers. You are just talking big.' (99)

Bama also speaks of Ambedkar and his philosophy, 'But Ambedkar was one of us, wasn't he? He struggled for the sake of our community, didn't he? Well? That's what these boys say; it is true?' (103)

Bama's main theme of *Sangati* is exploitation and marginalization of the Dalit women. She herself argues, 'Please don't say that, Amma. It is by repeating that to us that they have made us as useless as rotten eggs. Nowadays women can take up all sorts of responsibilities. But just as they fooled us and took away our rights within our homes, they have also marginalized us in the world outside. But now, generation by generation we must start thinking for ourselves, taking decisions, and daring to act. Don't we sharpen and renew a rusted sickle? Just like that, we must sharpen our minds and learn to live with self-respect.' (104)

It is pity that the upper-caste people misuse lower caste women but not the opposite as she writes, 'Well, if upper-caste men lay their hand on one of us, we might have to turn a blind eye out of fear, and let it go. But if Palla boys so much as touch paraiya girls or tease them, there always is terrible fight. Why are they prepared to fight then?' (106)

The suffering of a Dalit unmarried woman who is in need of a rent-house, is made to face a number of embarrassing questions. She makes a list of questions:

> They questioned me about my village, my name, my parents, and my brothers and sisters. Endless questions about my job, my property, my jewels, and each one of my belongings. I could never be at peace, thinking, 'All right, I have somehow managed to answer all their questions.' Because there was bound to be another spate of questions. What caste are you? What's your religion? Where do you work? How much do you earn? How old are you? Are you married? Why haven't you married yet? Are you going to marry at all? Why not? They will keep on pestering away like this. (120)

At the end of the novel Bama is more aggressive when she talks of the fate of all women; she is less worried about herself:

> But even though I think and agonize like this, I know that my own situation is not so bad. Somehow, I have a little education, I earn a living, and stand on my own two feet. But when I think of the women from my community who can't tell 'a' from 'aa,' and bend low to receive endless blows at home and at work, I am filed with frustration. When everything is added up and calculated, it seems to me that society is arranged as if God created women only for the convenience of men. In daily practice, women have to make sure that men don't suffer discomfort, that they are consoled and comforted, all their needs looked after, and all their bodily hungers

> satisfied. In short, they must be conscious every minute of their day that men are at the very centre of their lives. (122)
>
> Men can humiliate us a thousand times, speak about us with disrespect, and act toward us in that way too. And that is accepted as normal. But let a woman be outspoken just once-just one single time-let her act just once with self-respect. He will never stand for it. Until he has beaten her, broken her spirit, and gained control over her, he won't even digest his kanji. If a woman has gone beyond his controlling hand, his very moustache will begin to twitch. And if we become terrified and give in then we have to live and die like beasts of burden. (122)

Bama tries to give her own suggestions to curb this inhuman practice of exploiting Dalit women. She advocates as 'We should educate boys and girls alike, showing no difference between them as they grow into adults. We should give our girls the freedom we give our boys. If we rear our children like this from the time they are babies, women will reveal their strength. Then there will come a day when men and women will live as one, with no difference between them; with equal rights. Then injustice, violence, and inequalities will come to an end, and the saying will come true that 'Women can make and women can break.' Bama ends her very sad tale of the Dalit community with a positive note by saying, 'I am hopeful that such a time will come soon.'

A renowned writer with international repute R.K. Dhawan, sums up Bama's work *Sangati,* as '*Sangati* deals with several generations of women: the older women like the narrator's grandmother Vellaiamma, writer—her own self and the generation coming after her. The book is in the voices of many women speaking and addressing one another as they share the incidents of their daily lives. There is a special quality in these women. They may be oppressed and tortured, but they do not take things lying down. They are not simplistic; they are subtle women. They have the ability of undermining the authority figures by ridiculing them or playing tricks on them. They may be suffering but nonetheless they can laugh at their masters'[9]

Robert J.C. Young in his book *Postcolonialism* provides the reasons for treating women as different from men: 'Yet paradoxically, for women colonial ideology could represent new forms of freedom. As a result, women were much more ambivalently placed in relation both to colonialism and anti-colonial nationalism. This has also meant that while women struggle with the legacies of colonialism in the postcolonial era, they are repeatedly accused of importing western ideas. Well-meaning interventions by western feminists, human rights groups . . . all kinds comes from below rather than being imposed from above.'[10]

Bama intends to establish Dalit women empowerment through active participation and fighting against oppression of caste ideology of Hindus and orthodox attitudes of sin and expiation of Christianity. Her struggle is a message for the marginalized section of Dalit women to fight justice by resistance and reforming themselves through education.

The present piece of writing may be rightly concluded with objective observations and pertinent questions asked by Lind D. Molm and Mark Hedley in their *Gender, Power, and Social Exchange*: 'One of the most basic indicators of gender inequality is the distribution of power between men and women. Across time, across societies, and across a wide range of settings, men have greater power than women. They have greater access to, and control over, valued resources, and they have greater *formal* power, embedded in positions of authority and codified in law. At the macro level, this unequal distribution of power is a basic indicator of gender inequality. At the macro level, it raises questions about the relation between interaction and gender inequality. Are men more willing or more effective users of power than women, or do they simply appear so because of their greater access to structural power? Would gender-equal positions of structural power erase any gender differences in power-related interactions-exchange, cooperation, bargaining, and the like? Or do men and women use power differently even when their capacity for power use is equivalent?'[11]

Exploited class including women should make a strong fight to get justice and lead life meaningfully. Channappa makes the following observation about the revolution: 'Revolution would be impossible without the resolute self-confidence of the most to fight. No society is harmonious, classless and colourless. Every society is created with plurality of cultures and traditions. It is the common phenomenon of human society but it should generate equality, humanity, liberty and exploitation free society. The negative and inhuman elements should be eradicated. . . . Cursing and considering human birth itself as sinful and surrendering to the Creator is hypocrisy. And self-styled bloodshed revolutionaries, posing themselves as the protectors of poor and killing innocent people are really damaging the human relationship. The panacea for this problem is to follow the golden saying 'live' and 'let live.' It should be everyone's way of life. The human beings are responsible for all the ups and downs of the human society. The class system is the creation of immaturity of human beings. Maturity can cure these dreaded diseases.'[12]

Sangati is not just a creative work of pure imagination but it is culminated with the confluence of objective and subjective themes. Bama has very much succeeded by transforming individual predicaments into universal miseries and sufferings of women. This is one of the reasons the work *Sangati,* the 'community autobiography' of Bama demands further exploration of reading and understanding the deeper socio-economic issues of our society.

Works Cited

1. G. Baskaran, ed. *Alternate Identities: Essays on Commonwealth Literature,* Viking India, 2010, p. 7.3
2. *Ibid.*, p. 135.
3. *Ibid.*, p. 160.
4. http://en.wikipedia.org/wiki/Marxist. p. 14
5. Cecilia L. Ridgeway, ed., *Gender, Interaction, and Inequality,* Springer-Verlag, New York, 1991, p. 1.
6. C. Channappa, *Voices of Protest: The Fiction of Ngugi and C. Bharathi,* Prestige Books International, New Delhi, 2012, p. 151.
7. C. Channappa, *Indian and African Literature*, Prestige Books International, New Delhi; 2014, p.50
8. Channappa, *Ibid.*, pp. 15-16.
9. Mala Pandurang, *African Women Novelists: Re-Imaging Gender*, ed. Pencraft International, New Delhi, 2010.
10. Introduction to Bama's *Sangati,* Lakshmi Holmstrom: xii,7
11. Robert J.C. Young, *Postcolonialism,* Oxford University Press, New York, 2003, pp. 97-98.

Investigating Dalit Perspectives through Bama's *Vanmam* (Vendetta)

BOLLAVARAPU RAJU
Andhra Loyola College, Vijayawada

In India, caste ideology operates at a deeper level and in more complex ways than what we have realized so far. The dynamics of caste and Dalit issues are closely linked with our ideas of identity and the self. Bama's *Vanman* itself is the most forceful resistance to the caste-ideology that operates so vigorously in India. "When readers of communities other than my own read these palm-leaf manuscripts of mine, they will feel giddy, experience extreme palpitation in the heart, and intense, painful soreness in the eyes. And what is more they will unlearn everything. (N.D. Rajkumar, qtd. Azhagarasan xxvi) All Dalit writers in India wish that the people in India should show empathy with the pain of a Dalit. But to experience the pain of a Dalit what is needed is to 'unlearn' the typical and usual response that we give to the lived experiences of a Dalit. And unlearning anything is the most difficult thing, especially when a society has to unlearn something.

The dynamics of caste and Dalit issues are closely linked with our ideas of identity and the self. The caste-identity is something that defines our notions of self, subject, religion, culture and also everyday lived experience. The caste identity is something that we have historically inherited, learned and practiced for ages, and lived concretely for centuries. Caste is the basis of our consciousness, of our knowledge systems, and of course of our discourse practices which constitute our knowledge systems. Caste is our primordial being; our existential being cannot escape it. By paradigms of dominance, I mean the dominance of caste system and caste-structures that dominate our lives. The narratives of Dalit writings are also dominated by caste issues. "Caste as a cultural category, thus, becomes central to an understanding of Indian culture. This way of re-situating Ambedkar in the present theoretical context may help us trace the anti-caste framework found in the Dalit intellectual tradition and in also what emerges today as Dalit literature" (Azhagarasan xxii). However, resistance of caste is not something that is outside this dominance.

Dalit fiction, so far, as a category of writing that documents, foregrounds oppression of Dalits by upper castes, state and institutionalized religion. This form of exploitation extends to social, economic, political and sexual spheres of their life. In this context, both Dalit men and women, young or old, in rural milieu or in a metro are targeted without exception. Dalit women face discrimination on grounds of their caste identity, their oppression both at home and outside; gender adds another dimension to questions of identity and empowerment concerning Dalit community. The dual pressures of caste and gender place Dalit women in a specifically far more exploited matrix than their male counterparts. While sexual harassment, threat or fact of rape by upper castes or the police is a well-recognized form of oppression faced by Dalit women, what is less recognized is that the Dalit men subject their womenfolk to equally violent, sexually demeaning conduct. The position of women in a Dalit community is far more vulnerable than that of non-Dalit women in our society. Their impoverished economic condition only adds further misery to their subjugated position.

Bama's *Vanman* published in 2008 in Tamil, translated into English as *Vendetta* by Malini Seshadri, strikes a chord in Dalit writing. Unlike her earlier works and many of the Dalit writings, in *Vanmam,* Bama instead of blowing up the agonies and sufferings of the downtrodden, loudly raises her voice and vehemently asserts the need for the unity and solidarity of the suppressed for a better future. It is interesting that many of the writings of Bama have been translated into French before English. As Bama says, "Oh, the French have so much regard for literature. They appreciated my writing for its own quality. They didn't think 'she is a woman writer' or 'she is a Dalit.'" (*Vendetta,*" interview with the author, 156).

Bama writes about Dalit women in her novels in her capacity as a Dalit woman herself. She makes it evident that writing from the margin—the act of writing for a Dalit woman is a political act. She seeks to subvert dominant perception, representation and articulation of Dalit women's lives. In Bama's writings, there is a close link between education, writing and empowerment that Bama posits as tools that could liberate women of their caste.

Dalit literary writing is a mode of activism that seeks to free Dalits from the clutches of dominant ideology and 'casteist' oppression. This fiction argues for an activist intervention in the context of Dalit empowerment in Tamil Nadu. She believes that, "reading and writing are political practice" for a Dalit. She likes to foreground Dalits' resistance to oppression rather than merely record their victimization on account of their caste.

A Dalit is kept away from formal education due to social, economic and ideological paradigms. The Sanskritic tradition was totally inaccessible to a Dalit. Things have changed over the ages for Dalits in the Indian social milieu. In modern India, social prejudice and economic deprivation largely account for lack of educational opportunities for Dalits. In post-Independence India, the situation has not improved much indeed.

Vanmam deals with the internal animosity among Dalits in Tamil Nadu. It prevails not just in Tamil Nadu but in every state of India. Whether it is animosity between Dalits and the elite sections or Dalits with sub-sections, it is very pertinent to know that women are subjugated in every sphere of life both by men of upper caste and by their own men and her own community. The novel *Vendetta* is about animosity between two castes within Dalits. Pallars and Paraiyars are the two Dalit castes discussed in the novel. Pallars are recognized as Hindus and Paraiyars are Christian converts.

Bama belongs to the class of first generation learners in her community and has found a place in academic circles by virtue of being a school teacher and more significantly as a writer. She lays great emphasis on education as a means of social empowerment. As an activist writer, she forges close ideological affinity with feminist thought. Women and Dalits are both oppressed groups, oppressed on account of their birth. Bama foregrounds the affinity between the two groups and uses feminist strategies of representation, rereading and historicizing the oppression of in her narrative of Dalit experience. She points out in her writing that Dalits would have to help themselves and assert their difference from the dominant castes as a strategy of self-affirmation. She also writes about the Dalit in the Dalits' own vocabulary refusing to follow traditional notions of form, style, aesthetic paradigms or acceptable forms of diction and grammar. She seeks to represent women by tracing gaps in literary history, emphasizing difference as a principle of affirmation even if it is located as social advantage to the group. Bama affirms her Dalit identity and refuses to be accommodated into mainstream literary circles. Dalit writing in Tamil and Bama's in particular employs feminist thought and modes of resistance. Her works adopt a more militant framework as they break free from the shackles of upper middle class matrix that often invade literary discourse.

Bama's *Vanmam* has been described as "discourse of discontent," "a politics of difference" from mainstream feminism and it has been criticized for marginalizing Dalit women. Dalit feminist discourse questions Indian feminisms hegemony speaking about all women. According to Dalit feminists, "Dalit women are facing three way of oppression viz. caste oppression at the hands of upper castes-class based oppression at the hands of the upper and middle castes and as a women, who experience patriarchal oppression at the hands of all men and men of their own castes."

Bama's *Vanmam* is in many ways makes a marked departure from her earlier works *Karukku* and *Sangati.* Moving away from her earlier autobiographical mode, *Vanmam* steers clear of the familiar confessional, conversational tone and adopts a linear, descriptive, omniscient narrative. The narrative is less impassioned, less dramatic and often dull as compared to Bama's earlier works. Another marked characteristic of Bama's writing, her wit and bouncy humour, the celebratory resilience and earthy vigour of her characters and their vocabulary is also not evident in *Vanmam.* The self-effacing, omniscient narrator is also an implicated participant as evident in the pronounced empathy for Paraiyar victimhood in the unceasing strife between Pallars and Paraiyars that forms the subject of this novel. Bama's *Vanmam* raises an important aspect of Dalit life that has been less recognized and little acknowledged in Dalit writings in Tamil and Dalit studies at large. The fixing of Dalit as a homogenous, univocal category has largely governed the critical perspective on Dalit literary discourse in the last two decades. This inevitably led to easy vilification of Dalits and their writing whenever intra-Dalit strife took place or was written about. Even as Dalits were able to bargain better in the political domain, they were constrained to erase their cultural, community or vocation specific distinctiveness aspects that lent them individuality and self-esteem. In the late 1990s, Dalit writers began to display a sharper and more candid self-appraisal of Dalit subjectivity in the context of plurality and cultural/religious diversity amongst Dalits. Sivakami's very first novel, *Pazhiyana Kazidalum* (recently translated by the author as 'The Grip of Change' 2006) drew attention to the prevailing hierarchical social structure within Dalit communities. The novel published as early as 1989 (in Tamil) underlined the need for Dalits to mobilize themselves and sink their differences to be able to bargain for their rights better. Imayam's novels *Koveru Kazhudaigal* (1994) and *Arumugam* (1999) fore-grounded the dominance of a particular Dalit community over the other Dalit communities often resulting in a duplication of the hegemonic caste structure of Hindu society among Dalits and how this has percolated even amongst Dalits who have converted to Christianity. Imayam's novels received hostile criticism on account of their critique of Paraiyar's dominance over Dalit communities who stand further way below in the caste ladder.

In Bama's *Vanmam* there is intra-strife among Dalits which is discussed and strategies are debated to resolve the same. In many respects, *Vanmam* is a less intense or moving tale in comparison to *Karukku* and *Sangati*. Certain issues, even incidents narrated or discussed in her earlier works are taken up again in *Vanmam*, without however, adding a new or different dimension to the quality of discussion. Although Bama had employed repetition as a deliberate narrative strategy in *Karukku* and *Sangati*, she had used it to add a fresh interpretation or reveal another critical reading of the narrative material than given in her earlier treatment. This engaging trope is missing in *Vanmam*. Disappointing as this may be, a critical study of *Vanmam* is warranted as she subjects Dalits—both Paraiyars and Pallars—to an objective scrutiny and calls for forging of unity among Dalits on social and more significantly political grounds.

In *Vanmam*, the plot is a rather weak one as it merely dovetails the events involving two Dalit castes in a village called Kandampatti in Tamil Nadu which may be considered a microcosm of the Indian subcontinent. It is a village surrounded by beautiful mountains where people of different communities live for generations. The Paraiyars of the village are Christians and their Church is in the western part of the village. Next to the Paraiyar streets are the streets of Pallars who are also Dalits, but Hindus. Away from the Dalit streets are the streets of Naickers, Nadars, Thevars and Chettiars. Agricultural land owned by the landlords is in the western part of the village and therefore both Paraiyars and Pallars have to walk through the streets of the upper class to reach the fields. The Paraiyars and Pallars of the village are labourers in the fields of the landlords and they are destined to lead a pitiable existence with the husk thrown by them. In spite of their hard labour they have to remain half-fed with porridge. While commenting on the diligence of Paraiyars, Bama writers, "The Paraiyars toiled hard day and night to turn even barren land into fertile fields" (6). Azhagarasan's introduction rightfully points out to the lingering doubt that might rise in the reader about the authorial voice being caught up in the complexities of caste equation that she describes. "This is obvious in her [Bama's] construct of the subjugated, yet reasonable Paraiyar, and the cruel, insensitive Pallar," points out the introduction.

In the interview appended to the novel, Bama says, "the events I narrated in *Vanmam* are limited to a particular village. So, you cannot take it as a generalized statement." But it is difficult not to get into generalized conclusions. More so in translated texts. What one might sense while reading a text in Tamil with all its regional and caste variations of diction, usage and relationship among the speakers get lost in English.

Gail Omvedt, renowned Dalit studies scholar, in her review of *Vanmam*: "In almost every region of India there are two main (Dalit) castes, often at odds." (*Indian Express*, New Delhi, August 9, 2008). She actually formulates a whole dichotomous structure among Dalits religion and movement. *Vanmam* certainly has laid the ground open for such formulation, which is not only detrimental to Dalit struggles but also too simplistic.

Also, for reader's familiar with Bama's *Karukku* and *Sangati,* what is missing here is the powerful presence of gender. The women are in fringes, at a loss to have a say in this madness. What is worse is that they are not sure what to say or do. In fact, fights over space for women to relieve themselves and sexual abuses are showered on each other by the women of the respective communities.

While answering Azhagarasan's question on foregrounding "caste among women," Bama pitches "Dalit patriarchy and caste in feminist movements" as polarized arguments. She goes on to elaborate that "Dalit woman is not even considered as a 'subject' and caste was never considered to be a subject for discussion" in feminist circles. But right from early 1990s there have been concerted efforts among feminist thinkers and activists to construct the history of Dalit feminism in India. Sharmila Rege's *Writing Caste, Writing Gender and We also Made History: Women in Ambedkerite Movement* by Urmila Pawar and Meenakshi Moon (Trans. Wandana Sonalkar) are recent additions in that effort. In Tamil Nadu, one can confidently say that though casteism may not figure in the discourses among the ranks of women's movements and NGO activism, Dalit women's plight and their specific burdens have never been absent. It is unfortunate that a writer of Bama's calibre should close down the options of discussion. Polarizing Dalit feminism and critique of Dalit patriarchy does not help to unpack the complex relationship between gender and caste. In the process what escapes unaffected is an all pervasive masculinity in which Dalit males too have their stake.

Vanmam shares the discourse of modernity, addresses issues concerning contemporary society and its contradictions. (Introduction: 25) The crux of this novel can be understood in the author's own words, "marginalized people, those who have been pushed to the very edges of society, have to put aside their internal enmities if they are to reclaim their self-respect and their rightful place in society" (Author's note: 7) *Vanmam* is all about combating cruelties based on caste system with constructive strategy of empowerment.

Vanmam begins with a question, "Every human being should be seen as a human being, and respected as a human being. That is their goal . . . a society in which every person is equal. Will it ever be a reality?" (Author's note: 8) *Vanmam* is situated in the village called Kandampatti where people of different castes live. The houses of people are clustered based on the caste they belong to. The Paraiyars and Pallars live in the eastern part of the village. The children of both Paraiyars and Pallars go to schools. Most of the Pallars leave the village to get education: "As more and more of the Paraiyar boys left the village to get education and then came back, they began to detest this practice whole heartedly" (7). From this it can be understood that it is the education which made all the difference in their lifestyle. They wanted to improve their life style because they are able to ponder and realize what went wrong. In their heart of hearts they ask why god has made them like that, but made us like this, lower caste Dalits.

Vanmam delineates the story of Dalits and their struggle for existence. It is about the Dalits who struggled hard to live and survive in spite of several inhuman treatments meted out to them. It is the victory of the victimized over the caste based discrimination. Education played a crucial role in the change of the situation in the village where some of the educated people started their fight against this caste based politics played by the upper caste people. They also realized that the upper caste people use Dalits as pawns to instigate anger and fume among Dalits so that they can benefit from this policy of divide and rule. In the beginning, Dalits who led a peaceful life started fighting among themselves, instigated by the other caste people. This struggle for domination consumed lives of a number of innocent Dalits for no fault of theirs, made scapegoats most of the times.

This animosity continued for several years among Dalit communities in spite of several compromises.

Bama's heart seems to have pricked by the wretched and vulnerable condition in which Dalits live. In order to depict the real situation, she gives a glimpse of Saminathan's house which is a thatched house. They don't even have place to sleep properly in their house: "Not all of them can stretch out to sleep inside that tiny space. Usually, Saminathan and his father go to chavadi to sleep." (6). The condition of Dalits is low they don't even have two meals per day.

After completion of their lowly jobs they brought only Kanji and pickle to stay alive. Marrasu, a Parayan and Kuruppusamy, a Pallan earn their living by working in the fields of Naickers. There are frequent quarrels between Marraasu and Kuruppusamy, Pichamurthy, a Pallan helped them to understand that it is futile to fight for this, "Why all this fighting amongst us? Whether the fields are dry or watered, what is the gain to you? It's someone else who is going to reap the benefit, but it's you two who are fighting! Let it go both of you" (10). As things took its worst stage Kuruppusamy lifted the spade he was holding, and with the shaft of the spade he struck hard blow on the head of Marraasu. Marraasu fell to the ground with a cry of utmost agony. Saminathan felt distressed whenever he thought of how his uncle Marraasu had been murdered. The memory also aroused and insane fury in him. "Because we have no money, no education, they killed and buried Chithappa in a ditch. . . . As if it was all in a day's work, as if he were a mere dog or something" (11). In another episode, Pallars killed Sethurathnam and Savariappan. The horrible scene of Sethurathnam being chased and hacked to death still lingered in the minds of Paraiyars.

Mekalamma, one of the Paraiyar women, made a very true and interesting point about all these fights among these two Dalit groups: "they're the ones who are plotting to make sure our two castes never unite. This has been going on for ten or twenty years now" (12).

The vendetta between the Paraiyars and Pallars does not have a valid reason and its source is not clearly known. The earliest instance of violence is the killing of a Pallar by a Parayan named Mannangati. Mannangati enjoyed certain privileges in the village which irked the Pallars who out of envy dragged him to a brawl and tried to stab him. But Mannangati got hold of the knife and ripped out the guts of a Pallar. Yet the Parayas and Pallars get along well. On another occasion, Marraasu, a Paraiyar and Karuppuswamy, a Pallar, got into a quarrel when both were involved in watering the farms of Naicker. Following the instigation of the landlord who encouraged him "to be aggressive and promised to take care of everything" (8). Karuppuswamy killed Marraasu. These are isolated incidents which do not affect the cordial relationship between the Parayas and Pallars and they celebrated festivals together and took part in common functions and programmes. By the time some of the educated youths of Paryar streets formed the "Kalani Arts Club" and conducted various cultural events. These developments on the Paraiyar street make the Naickers jealous and they accused the church for encouraging the Paraiyars. "They belong to the Church, they get lots of support. Also, many of them are now educated" (2). Strengthened by the successful conduct of cultural programmes, the Dalit youngsters wanted to install a statue of Ambedkar. Further, they desired the involvement of all Dalit groups in the venture. The Pallars donated Rs.1,000 for the statue, which was unveiled in a colourful function. The solidarity in organizing the programme and the speeches made on the occasion infuriated the landlords who conspired to annihilate the unity of the downtrodden. Goaded by the Naickers, some of the Pallars demanded the return the money donated for the statue. The corporate life of the Paraiyars and Pallars faced a serious setback over the issue of putting up a flagpole near the statue of

Ambedkar. Violence erupted when a wire tied to the pole was cut by a Paraiyar young man. Instead of pacifying, the landlords instigated the Pallars. "How arrogant they are to lay a hand on the wire you people have put there. Don't let them get away with this. It's either you or them now" (80).

In the violence that followed, innocent people from both sides were mercilessly butchered and houses and belongings were destroyed. The worst affected by the violence were Parayas who could not get support either from the Government or from the Church, whereas the Pallars enjoyed the favours of the landlords and police. The Paraya men dispersed to different places out of fear. Under the guise of searching for men, police "enter the house of Parayas and talk vulgarly to the women and even misbehaved with them" (88).

The women were dragged to street and they were beaten brutally, "with no regard even for the infant and the aged, they kept and swirling their lathis down hard again and again" (89). They got blown everywhere in their bodies: "All the women had swellings and black bruises all over their bodies as the blood clotted and congealed under the blows" (89).

The Paraiyar women were more scared of the police than of the riots. The women who were taken to the police station were subjected to more severe torture and abuses. Chellakili, a pregnant Paraiyar woman was kicked in the lower belly by a policeman with his boot: "Chellakili curled up and collapsed on the floor of the cell. As she lay there on the floor of that police lock-up, she felt a sharp pain in her belly . . . and had an abortion right there" (86).

Kandampatti was under the grip of fear. The following year the Paraiyars had to skip Christmas celebration. However, during the Easter festivities violence broke out in the village. The loss of lives, oblique poverty and tormenting experiences of violence make the villagers brood over the destructive nature of vendetta which makes them realize that nothing can be achieved through violence. They could not harvest anything but the loss of a few innocent lives, untold miseries and misfortunes.

For the upper class Naickers, "the news that the Paraiyar street had become a wasteland was as sweet as the sweet of nectar" (122). When the murder of a Paraya came to trial in the Court of Law there evolved a common notion of peace between the two communities. Jayaraju, an educated Paraiyar young man, declared in public, "we were just beginning to progress slowly and now three murders and court cases and police raids . . . all over people scattered about, studies ruined, not even able to attend Church . . . how long can we go on like this? (126). The two groups resumed discussion which led to a compromise between them. They unanimously declare, "After all, life is short. We work, we eat . . . we die. Why take on unnecessary problems?" (129). When the upper class people heard of a peace agreement, they mocked and ridiculed both Pallars and Paraiyars: "What sort of fellows are these? After so much killing . . . so much wandering around like refugees . . . they are supposed to be uniting again. Shameless fellows!" (132).

In fact, the upper class people are upset over the unity of the subaltern as they are quite sure that their domination will be questioned. Bama has quite an optimistic vision of a very bright future for the Dalits. She finds a zest for life, amazed at the courage of the Dalits and is astonished at the resilience of the Dalit women, in particular. There is a burning desire to develop and a thirst for knowledge prevails among the Dalit youths. When the men were hiding to avoid arrest, the Paraya woman stayed indoors. They carried on the routine work and withstood police brutality and threats. "Though misfortunes and problems continued to pile up, the women faced them all resourcefully" (123). There is yet another incident in the novel where the Dalit women themselves received the corpse of three persons killed in the violence. Bama enters a highly problematic area of inequality and violence between various Dalit communities.

Vanmam documents hatred and vengeance among the various Dalit communities, an area too touchy to be addressed and too complex to be grasped. It is sad but true that the graded inequality that sustains caste order is replicated among the Dalits as well. The hierarchy among Dalits in Tamil Nadu has the following structure as a given: Pallar, Paraiyar and Arundathiyar. The novel has chosen to deal with the top two castes among the Dalits and not the hierarchically positioned Arundathiyar, for example. The idyllic bonding between the two communities built through cultural events, sports and celebration of festivals turns out to be a mere façade to mask the burning jealousies over socio-economic issues. Unfortunately, conversion to Christianity becomes the key variable in causing this divide. The bloody caste clashes begin with a Hindu Pallar murdering a Christian Paraiyar. The story ends with the murder of an innocent Paraiyar that leads to the dawn of realization among both the parties about how they have been made pawns in the hands of caste Hindus. Finally a resolution is sought in electoral politics.

Vanmam shows how Dalits have internalized the given social system of segregation based on caste. If Paraiyars and Pallars are outcastes in the eyes of Naickers, Odaiyars, Chettiars, Naidus and Nadars; Pallars and Paraiyars treat each other as outcastes within their own social habitat. While Paraiyars have embraced Christianity, Pallars remain within the Hindu fold. This fact is played up by Naickers and other upper castes to keep the two Dalit communities divided. This results in Paraiyars and Pallars getting into arguments and tiffs over whose lands should be watered first. While Paraiyars and Pallars remain landless, they go to the extent of killing each other over an argument over whose landlord's lands are irrigated better. The novel in fact opens with an account of murder of a Paraiyar farmhand, Mariyasu at the hands of Karupasami, a Pallar farmhand, over distribution of water to their respective master's lands. As Karupasami's master protects him, he gets away with Mariyasu's murder and surreptitious disposal of his body. In this way, the enmity between the two communities is nurtured and kept alive by Naickers: "God knows when we, Paraiyars and Pallars, would stand united," exclaims a Paraiyar women, Mekalamma. Mekalamma's lament becomes the central refrain of the novel. One incident leads to the other. If a member from the Pallar community becomes the aggressor in one incident, a Paraiyar becomes the aggressor in another. The upper caste landlords stoke the fire of hatred and prejudice, call in the police and settle scores with the Paraiyars. The novel is written from the Paraiyar's point of view although an objective analysis is undertaken to demonstrate that Pallars are used by Naickers for their own political gain. The rest of the novel deals with bloody caste clash, forcing men to hide. Children are forced to remain at home. High castes and police officials put oil to the fire and ultimately women are widowed and children are orphaned.

The Paraiyar community, thanks to education accessible through missionary-run schools, is considered advanced socially and economically. There is a greater political awareness among them and they are highly resented by upper castes for emulating Ambedkarite thought. The novel depicts how Paraiyar youth, most of them college-educated, pursuing a post-graduate degree, organize cultural activities, sports competitions and awareness campaigns to spread Ambedkar's thought in their community, when they return home from their hostels during vacations. Hope for political unity among Dalits lies with this segment. Pallars are mostly school dropouts and their youth are shown to be either working for Naickers or unemployed but always envious of their Paraiyar counterparts. But despite the best efforts of Paraiyar youth, caste strife between the two communities does not get stalled, resulting in rampant police brutality, forcing young men and adult males to either flee and live incognito or rot in jails.

Paraiyar youth, although they fashion themselves as radical, are yet orthodox in their attitude towards their women. After the cultural programme, the young men want to hold a meeting at the chavadi to discuss future action plan. But they do not invite or want women to be present. Jayarasu announces: "We shall continue with our cultural program. As a meeting is scheduled to be held at chavadi, women are asked to return to their homes quietly" (80). The educated girls protest, but to no avail. Selvarani observes: "These boys call themselves great reformists. But if there is a 'village meeting,' they ask us, women, to go home. What kind of justice is this?" (80). Older women explain to the girls, "Oh, come on, Men shall be men and women shall remain women." (80)

Three young Paraiyar boys, Paulraju, Saharaju and Panner Selvam are more frenzied with every passing day. They were the people who had run away when Sesuratnam was attacked. They went about with only one constant thought in their mind, i.e. to carry out revenge by killing Pallans: "For those two or three weeks, people went about nervously: not knowing what would happen or when. Then, just as things seemed to be somewhat settling Back to normal . . . suddenly, totally unexpectedly . . . it happened." (114)

The moment they caught sight of three or four Pallans, they thought they should finish them off. They whipped out their arrivals and hacked down Pallans. After this incident Pallans waited with blood lust to take revenge. Since Pallans were not able to get hold of any Paraiyar man the Pallar people, "With a single blow one of them chopped off Chandan Mary's head. They hacked down Amal or Bhavam even as she pleaded for mercy, palms pressed together. . . . Amalor Bhavam fell to the ground unconscious" (12). So many incidents were occurred in the lives of the Pallavans and Paraiyars. These fights and revenges posed a serious threat to their lives and their existence seem to be a big question mark to them. They rarely realize that they are fighting for their masters and killing their own brothers and sisters. This realization had made all the change in the lives of Paraiyars and Pallars. They realized that it "started as a small spark now its raging flame that is threatening to burn us all" (127).

When Sethuratnam's murder case came up for hearing Paraiyars, found it difficult to pursue the case in the situation in which they were in and Pallars realized that the accused Pallans would be convicted of the murder so they thought they should settle the matter amicably. This helped them to realize that, "We want to live like human beings. But if we were treated like beasts, we may have to act like situation demands . . . others live first and then die; but we are dying even when we're still alive. At least the generations to come must live well. Let's find a way to do that, said naattaamai firmly" (130).

The constant message from the elders of the both the streets, "what's past is past. But the children who are yet to born must be able to live in this village. So, let's trust one another and try to get along together" (134). This realization made them to settle for a compromise. This hard struck compromise among these two Dalit groups rang a death bell in the minds and hearts of the Naickers who were obsessed with the power and snatched power away from them. At last, when their candidate Kaalaiyan, who was selected by both Pallavans and Paraiyars, got elected as the President, people of both the communities went to the Panchayat office, which alarmed the Naickers. This marked the victory of the Dalits over the domination of the upper caste people which was possible only after the loss of several great and innocent Dalits. This code of compromise is the result of education combined with experience. It can be affirmed that Dalits can raise their standards only by education which can dismantle the shackles of caste based discrimination which treat humans as some entities with no individuality.

Vanmam, through fights, fumes, animosities, combats and compromises, presents a realistic portrayal of life and struggle of Dalits and is a bidding farewell to the age old venomous practices of the upper caste people. It is a lesson to all Dalits who fight among themselves in the oblivion that united they stand divided they fall. It is the struggle for the existence which made Pallavans and Paraiyars to fight among themselves. But as the dawn of realization struck the chord of compromise, they understood that their struggle to raise the standards of their life style can only be a meaningful endeavour "as Ambedkar, the champion of the downtrodden, said, we must capture the levers of government power" (134). The escalation towards a better life is possible only if Dalits "Educate! Organize! Agitate!

In the last chapter of this novel, *Vanmam*, there are answers to the questions that are raised by Bama in the author's note of the novel, "Let the coming generations at least live without quarrels end, fights, riots and vendettas. Let them get along with one another . . . as for the future . . . along with the hope there also lurks the old fear. But, in their minds, they know clearly what they have to do . . . where they want to go" (135). *Vanmam* ends on a note of enlightenment that 'united they stand and divided they fall.'

Vanmam is for forging unity among Dalits. Education for Bama is not limited to formal education. She lays equal emphasis on spiritual education but wants this to be free from interference from ecclesiasts and officialdom. Dalits have to gain enlightenment in a political sense, rather than merely accumulate university degrees. Bama's works coincide with the Ambedkarite vision for Dalit empowerment. If *Karukku* upholds education, *Sangati* foregrounds organized agitation, while *Vanmam* enjoins upon unity among Dalit communities.

Works Cited

Bama. *Vanmam*. Trans Malini Seshadri. New Delhi: OUP, 2008.

Bama. *Sangati*. Trans. Laxmi Holmstrom. New Delhi: OUP.2005.

Brent. *India: Incidents in the Life of a Slave Girl*. New York: Harcourt.1973.

Dumont, Louis. *Homo Hierarchicus: The Caste System and its Implications*. London: Paladin.1972.

Deshpande, L.S. "Dalit Poetry." *Dalit Literature and African American Literature*, ed. N.M. Aston, pp. 59-72.

Kolekar, N. Tanaji. *Authenticity of Dalit Experience and Literary Expression*, 2011.

Massey, James. *Downtrodden: The Struggle of India's Dalits for Identity, Solidarity and Liberation*. Geneva: WCC. 1997.

Rode, Sonali. *A Brief Study of Dalit Literature after 1960s*. International Research Journal. 2010.

Waghmare. "Literature of Marginality." *Dalit Literature and African American Literature*, ed. N.M. Aston. New Delhi: Prestige, 2001. pp. 16-24.

Amitav Ghosh and the Idea of Transnationalism

TUHINA BOSE
Fr. C. Rodrigues Institute of Tech., Navi Mumbai, Vashi

As the world today struggles to reconcile inherent differences with the inevitable proximity and commonality that the digital and media resources are gradually bringing in transnationalism has become a feature in many of the literary writings. The whole genre of the postcolonial studies though engaging in the identity crisis, addresses the issue of emergence and acceptance of transnationalism. In search for their identities, the liminal beings who cut across various frames of references emerge as phoenixes from the charred pieces of identification. It is important to understand and uncover the above sentiment because it is perhaps the most emotional part of the diasporic dilemma that lies unaddressed.

Transnationalism, as we know, is a much contested term in the globalized world of today, owing to its inflated overuse across the disciplines. It is "a multifaceted, multi-local process" (Guarnizo & Smith 6) that broadly denotes the "processes by which immigrants forge and sustain multi-stranded social relations that link together their societies of origin and settlement" (Basch, Glick Schiller and Szanton Blanc 6). Theorists like Portes argue that transnational practices are performed by non-institutional actors such as individual migrants and civil society actors "outside the realms of state regulation and control" (qtd. Morales and Jorba 269). Although such connections and exchanges did exist in the past, they have been accelerated by globalization and the resultant developments in trade, transport and communication systems across the world.

The concept of trans-nationalism refers to multiple ties and interactions linking people and institutions across the borders of nation-states. Trans-national activities can be defined as "those that take place on a recurrent basis across national borders and that require a regular and significant commitment of time by participants. Such activities may be conducted by relatively powerful actors, such as representatives of national governments and multinational corporations, or may be initiated by more modest individuals, such as immigrants and their home country kin and relations. These activities are not limited to economic enterprises, but include political, cultural and religious initiatives as well."

This definition indicates the close relationship between trans-nationalism and globalisation, which also refers essentially to the rapid expansion of cross-border transactions and networks in all areas of life. At the same time, the concept suggests that boundaries between nation-states are becoming less distinct.

Trans-national communities do not necessarily refer only to migrants, since cross-border groups with common cultural, sporting, political or other interests might also consider themselves a community. However, in practical terms, groups arising from migrations are the most significant type, and most research on trans-national communities refer to these. Clearly, migrants have always lived in more than one setting, maintaining links with a real or imagined community in the state of origin. The new is the context of globalisation and economic uncertainty that facilitates the construction of social relations transcending national borders. The increase in mobility and the development of communication have contributed to such relations and created a transnational space of economic, cultural and political participation.

The assumption that people will live their lives in one place, according to one set of national and cultural norms, in countries with impermeable national borders, no longer holds. Rather, in the 21st century, more and more people will belong to two or more societies at the same time. This is what many researchers refer to as transnational migration.

Through this paper I have tried to focus on the various international activities during the imperial era and how these became the very core of transnationalism and globalization much a part of our lives today. It is a study of a select novels of Amitav Ghosh where I have emphasized more on the study of the *Trilogy*, that is, *The Sea of Poppies*, *The River of Smoke and The Flood of Fire;* through this study I have brought out the perspectives in Ghosh's novels that are akin transnationalism that is, mainstreaming the marginalized, minimization of the requirement of borders; the human ability to surpass the territorialisation and highlighting the role of the marginalized in creating a space for the 'other'; thus rewriting the past. This facet has been explored very methodically in the narratives of Amitav Ghosh and these narratives convey a very deep understanding of the way societies are functioning in the contemporary set up. The paper would take up the aspects of historiography and culture to locate the emergence of transnationalism in literature

'It has been a practice since Immanuel Kant to isolate cultural and aesthetic realms from the worldly domain, it is time now to rejoin them.' (*Culture and Imperialism*). Said points out that a reconciliation has been reached between the haves and the have-nots, and this is visible as a process in many of the narratives of the diasporic literature, Amitav Ghosh being prominent amongst them.

The *Trilogy* is a metafiction, where the story of the colonization is woven in to bring out the minute details of the sufferings of the marginal, however it is woven in a postmodern tone to show that this whole process of suffering and adjustment changed the world structure altogether. The age of modernization and eulogization of the national was not important anymore; rather the quest for identity and recognition of the heterogeneous was more important.

These are all efforts to show, that the sentiments of globalization, as they transformed the world to its present form, existed within the purview of imperialism, the empire shifting its subjects here and forth. 'This pattern of dominion laid the groundwork for what in effect is today a fully global world.' (*Culture and Imperialism*)

Transnationalism became much a part of literature with characters like Raju, Zachary. Paulette, Freddie. The trilogy is a metafiction which reflects the adaptations and adjustments made by the characters in order to accommodate in the new world order. Through his various novels Ghosh dissects the sentiments pervading the world order. In the wake of mainstreaming the marginalized, Ghosh emphasizes on the aspect of local becoming global. In saying so it may be evident that the marginalized are pushed to the edge and thus to safeguard their existence they either adapt to or struggle against the existing norms. These two processes form the very core of the process of transnationalism.

In the study of novels that I have undertaken in this paper most of the characters are 'the other' and they struggle to crystallize their misshapen identity. In this regard people go through many upheavals of emotions. Ghosh addresses the issues of nostalgia, identity and citizenship in these novels. The evolution and ripening of the various facets of transnationalism happen in every nook and cranny of the characters' lives and Ghosh rewrites history taking the perspective of these marginalized beings; his novels revolve around the cultural comingling; unlearning the old and learning the new and in the process creating a different society. This is carried out by narrating each component's life in elaboration thus delineating the whole process of globalization and transnationalism. What Ghosh has done is comparable to the great historians like Herodotus but he does it with ardour of re-writing the past. His works form volumes of the historiographical records as he narrates the unexposed which by and large covers a large aspect of the marginalized taking over the main space.

Touching the above sentiments at their core, he has invoked these feelings in his writings and among the readers by laying out history as it occurred in the lives of the people. As History is not only a record of information it is a realization of the change; how and when it is happening. This phenomenon is laid out distinctly in the oeuvre of his works, thus making a transnational work possible on the platform of literature.

Thus, in the novels like the Trilogy, imperialistic imposition on the subjects and their going through a hazardous journey of life-changing events; rajah Neel and the captive together in the ship cabin . . . the cabin crew that consisting of a motley of people from different streams; in *The Hungry Tide*, Piyali's coming to Sunderbans researching the Irrawady dolphins, and seeking help from 'Fokir,' the bucolic boatman all builds up to the realization of a paradigm change that is taking place in the society.

'And so we felt silent, each of us alone with our thoughts. . . . I saw them coming, young and old quick and halt with their lives bundled on their heads, and knew it was of them the poet had spoken when he said, each slow turn of the world carries such disinherited ones to whom neither the past nor the future belong.' (*The Hungry Tide*). Such sentiments express the habits, rituals and social making of the transnational and are constantly occurring in various novels of Ghosh

In *The Hungry Tide*, 'Fokir' & 'Piyali' become one in thought and in transcending nature, another social order is broken when these two face the rigours caught on a lonely island amidst massive tidal wave. They are one in their pursuit and in understanding the sea and respecting its anguish. Piya feels more at home with Fokir than with Kannai although she is a cosmopolitan being. To present Piya in resonance with Fokir than with Kannai is an aberration and an effort. It is also an indication of the fact that realization of each other's emotions does not require a similar social status or background. The sea becomes a borderless territory reminding the readers that this world is seamless, that human intellect is a universal treasure to be used for human cause. Thus Fokir is brought in, in a very different light where he is more effective than Kannai at sea. His education might not be formal but he is the most valuable help that Piyali could avail. The macrocosmic form of the universe resonates with the human thinking in being unbound and it is not to be destroyed for petty misunderstandings. Piyali and Fokir are vivid examples of the transnational sentiments which a global being goes through.

Transnationalism is not an event, it is a phenomenon, a gradual process of evolution. This understanding is given to us by Ghosh through his various works. The idea takes shape in many of his narratives. These connect the local world with the global as is viewed in the character of 'Rajkumar,' Dinu and the king of Ratanagiri in the narrative, *The Glass Palace.* This address is always accompanied by the symbolic element in the backdrop, that which is universal, omnipresent reminds us of the connect that micro and macrocosmic elements would always eventually have. 'The world was formed by God and divided by humans.' The author deliberately throws his character into situations where each of them is forced to think beyond the social and physical barriers, and thus emerge victorious and 'mutated' as 'the global beings.'

Ghosh's latest trilogy is a continuation of this thought process, where the human intellect is given a panoramic understanding, not limiting it to nations, races and colour, rather mainstreaming the marginalized. The novel transcends space and borders, and while narrating the mind of the characters become the fertile ground for all the changes, for instance Deeti and Kalua, both go through the acid test of being treated inhumanly but they escape their destiny and rebuild a new world.

Ghosh builds a backdrop of the pre-independence times, assigning voices to different unrecognized characters. These voices seem to come from the chthonic undercover—the ignored, the neglected, and the oppressed. Destiny throws some of them together. On *Ibis* for example the ill-fated ship, the 'girmitiyans,' 'rajah Neel,' the convict, are all out to try their luck on a new land. Thus starts the journey of the unrecognized. Although these dislocated beings have no land to call their own, they become one in the agony of 'not belonging,' starting the creation of a new habitat. Jodu and Paullette, Deeti & Kalua, Mr. Reid all will eventually become the citizens of the new land. The ship serves to melt down their complexes and emerge as the phoenixes of the new world.

With a broader perspective Ghosh brings out that in the wake of imperial power struggle, the churning that took place left many, homeless dislocated and dispossessed. However, maintaining a forward-looking attitude, Ghosh does not pine and heave for what is lost, he rather engages in the creation of the new. His characters go through a partial amnesia, while the past stays, it does not hamper in the fresh life which is in the formation.

Ibis in the vast ocean, Fokir, Kannai & Piya in the tidal wave, Deeti and her companions emerging as powerful community in foreign land, May and Tridib falling in love despite India in the pre-independence era and full of anti-British sentiment, life finds a way to grow and evolve. Thus national is forgotten and transnational emerges.

Juxtaposing the idea against the digital wave that the world is going through, it seems that Ghosh understands transnationalism as a natural and confirmed evolutionary process in the history of mankind. In doing so, Ghosh traverses between postcolonialism and postmodernism. He is an amphibian who has extended the vistas of the postcolonial to overlap with the postmodern. His works talk about the postcolonial man. The novels are timed and spaced in the past but what emerges in the characters is very recent, a very postmodern trait, 'A transnational man in the making.' He irons out the past and renders it possible for his readers to understand how this was always charted in the map of global history. There were forces resisting it but they were rendered powerless in course of time.

The overlap of postmodern and transnational is noticed and acknowledged by many critics especially those who realize that while 'nation state' as a theory was popularized in the modern age, accepting a fragmented but wholesome world became an icon of the postmodern world. The characters seem to search for their identity and are ready to give up on their nameless and meaningless existence for an honest recognition.

'The intertextual parody of historiographic metafiction enacts, in a way, the views of certain contemporary historiographers (see Canary and Kozicki): it offers a sense of the presence of the past, but this is a past that can only be known from its texts, its traces--be they literary or historical.' (Linda Hutcheon). This is what Ghosh does precisely; he juxtaposes transnational sentiments against the backdrop of history, in a way telling his readers the perspective to look at history, reshaping their minds.

Thus Deeti, Putli, Kalua, Jodu, Mr. Reid, in the *trilogy*, Fokir & Piya in *The Hungry Tide*, May and Tridib in *The Shadow Lines*, materialize these transnational characters appreciate their existence and go all out to make it meaningful instead of giving up on life. Land and place do not matter, what matters is the sentimental connect and the identity of the self. The pain of dislocation and dispersal materializes into beings that have used the power of their sorrow to construct a stronger self, of course, supported by their adopted nations, thus becoming the rightful citizens 'there & here.'

Amitav Ghosh voices an ongoing phenomenon world over. His works are a recital of the past and the future of the nations, transnations and the transnationals. Embedded at the core of his narratives is the idea of a myriad, variegated and motley world with rainbow hues.

The process of merging worlds in the third trilogy is quite vivid; as Neel writes 'the shared secret of our escape from the *Ibis* has become a link between who we were then and who we are now; between past and present. It is a bond more powerful than ties of family and friendship. 'Jodu and Neel are two people from completely different backgrounds caught in the stereotype of hierarchy in India, but the moment of agony, of being the subalterns the dispossessed binds them into one thread they are out to traverse the global world all by themselves.'

One notices that the characters shaped up in the novels of Amitav Ghosh definitely transcend the national and become global; for that matter Zachary Reid, is one person who is neither completely an English nor completely an Indian. The insult he receives at the hands of Capt. Mee when *Ibis* is about to reach China points out how a person like Zachary negotiates multiple identities—his transnational self in making.

In a similar fashion Jodu comes across Muslims from all over the world in the Nanhae prison, 'there were Muslims from other places too, in and around China—Turks and Uzbegs, Malays and Arabs.' The oneness that these prisoners feel in being Muslims makes them surpass the fact that they are not in their own land, it is the beginning of a different world; whatever might be the reason for their unification. In fact imperial law and inhuman atrocities gave people a second chance to coexist. Singapore and Hongkong are the centres of international trade; traders from all over the world gather here. As Freddie mentions: 'You know why they come? Because this is "free port"—they pay no duties or taxes.' 'Opium pays for everything.' The shipmates who keep meeting; now they have a different identity; culture common to the bearers of the ship. The ocean defines their belongingness fraternity existence. The ocean becomes the hub of all cultural exchange. Deeti embraces Kalua and Neel and the convict are one in their dispossession—all looking for a respectful cohabitation. Paullette becomes Putli, in a sari she can hide her true identity; in doing so she partly adopts the cultural sensibilities of Deeti and other Indian women; she becomes one with them.

Also, the opium market where Reid and babu Nobo Kishen are investing the motley that is visible consists of people from all over the world. The whole culture is governed by the politics of opium trade. The imperial hegemony where the Chinese are compelled to buy opium and the motley of crowd consisting of Spanish Arab Turks Uzbek is a sight much akin to the transnational world today. The Streets like Colaba Causeway and Grant Road in Bandra present a scene no less than this. The exchange in the diasporic community is two way and what remains is the new concretized experience to be carried forward for the future generations. As Edward Said points out, 'the historical sense involves a perception, not only of the pastness of the past, but of its presence. The main idea is even as we fully comprehend the pastness of the past there is not just way in which past can be quarantined from the present.' Thus in the diasporic literature, more so in the novels of Ghosh, one finds the rewritten past like the changed history.

The most striking example comes from *The Flood of Fire* where Raju, Neel's son, who has been brought up in luxury, goes through a complete change when he becomes a fife at *Hind* and then at *Ibis*, his life is completely transformed. Raju is in a different land looking for his father, his friend Dick is the one who teaches him the way of life on the ship. At one point Raju mentions about the music lessons and immediately feigns a story of being someone's apprentice lest he gets pointed out as the privileged one. Raju's learning is about negotiating a culturally alien world, and creating a space for self; by becoming the boy for Zachary Reid he transcends his learning to global. As Said quotes in *Culture and Imperialism* 'Cultural experience or indeed every cultural form is radically quintessentially hybrid.'

The changing world order has come up with the sentiments which are culturally hybrid, as pointed out by Rushdie in *Imaginary Homelands* that the centre has shifted; now the narratives are being written by the multicultural transnational beings who govern the centre-space in literature. Said observes in this regard: 'It is difficult to connect these different realms to show the involvement of culture with expanding empires, to make observations about art that preserve its unique endowments and at the same time map its affiliations, but I submit we must attempt this and set the art in the global, earthly context.' The earth is in effect one world, in which empty uninhabited spaces virtually do not exist.

Works Cited

Agrawal, Devyani. Un-Essentializing Marginality in *Sea of Poppies*. www.museindia.com

Bose, Brinda. *Footnoting History: The Diasporic Imagination of Amitav Ghosh*, ed. Makarand Paranjape. New Delhi: India Log, 2001.

Bhabha, Homi. *The Location of Culture*. New York: Routledge, 1994.

Chakrabarty, *Dipesh. Provincializing Europe: Postcolonial Thought and Historical Difference*. New York: Princeton UP, 2000.

Dixon, Robert. "Travelling in the West: The Writing of Amitav Ghosh." *Amitav Ghosh: A Critical Companion*. Delhi: Permanent Black, 2003.

Fanon, Franz. *The Wretched of the Earth*. Grove Press, 1963.

Ghosh, Amitav. *Sea of Poppies*. New Delhi: Penguin, 2008.

_____. *Shadow Lines*. Oxford University Press, 1995.

_____. *Flood of Fire*. Penguin, 2015.

_____. *River of Smoke*. Penguin, 2011.

_____. *The Hungry Tide*. Harper Collins. 2005.

Grewal, Inderpal. "Amitav Ghosh: Cosmopolitanisms, Literature, Transnationalisms." *The Postcolonial and the Global*, ed. Revathi Krishnaswamy and John C. Hawley. Minneapolis: U of Minnesota P, 2008.

Hall, Stuart. "Cultural Identity and Diaspora." *Identity: Community, Culture, Difference*, ed. J. Rutherford. London: Lawrence and Wishart, 1990.

Rushdie, Salman. *Imaginary Homelands—Essays and Criticism*. Vintage, 2010.

Spivak, Gayatri Chakravarty. *In Other Worlds: Essays in Cultural Politics*. London: Routledge, 1988.

Said, Edward W. *Culture and Imperialism*. Vintage, 1993

Smith, Michael Peter and Guarnizo, Luis Eduardo. *Transnationalism From Below*. Transaction Publishers, 2009.

Linda Hutcheon, *Historiographic Metafiction: Parody and the Intertextuality of History*.

Postcolonial Consciousness: Amitav Ghosh's *The Calcutta Chromosome*

N. THYAGARAJU
S.A.S Degree College, Vijayawada

The novel in the postcolonial world is the result of a political phenomenon. Colonization is viewed as a system of political, economic, psychological and culture domination of one country over the other. It always ends in cultural and politics marginalization of the colonized country.

Further, colonization establishes a myth of intellectual, social, cultural, religious and physical snobbery and inferiority of the colonized. It distorts the native history and emasculates the voice of the oppressed. In the process of colonization, the victim may not curse but being aware of the weaknesses of the victimized, discloses them to establish his identity.

The postcolonial consciousness has created a necessity to have a plurality of voices as both the colonized and the de-colonized are seized by a 'double consciousness.' This double-consciousness of the postcolonial writer makes her reject and accept the dynamics of power knowledge nexus controlled by the imperialistic country. Bill Ashcroft in *The Empire Writes Back* states: "The term postcolonial applies to all the cultures affected by the imperial process from the moment of colonization to the present day. . . . In postcolonial studies, particularly in culture studies, colonized society pre-eminently absorbs a psychology that is concurrently pre-colonial, and postcolonial experience."

Ghosh's first novel, *The Circle of Reason* deals with the arrival of a child in a small village. The second novel, *The Shadow Lines,* focuses on the narrator's family in Calcutta and Dhaka and their connection with an English Family in London and *The Calcutta Chromosome* brings together three searches:

> The first is that of an Egyptian clerk, Antar, working alone in a New York apartment in the early years of the twenty-first century to trace the adventures of L. Murugan, who disappeared in Calcutta in 1995. The second pertains to Murugan's obsession with the missing links in the history of malaria research. The third search is that of Urmila Roy, a journalist in Calcutta in 1995 who is researching the works of Phulboni, a writer, who produced a strange cycle of 'Laakhan Stories' that he wrote on the 1930s but suppressed thereafter.

The novel *The Calcutta Chromosome* is not merely a science fiction exploring the mysterious ways of the supposed influences in the fact-finding journey in the course of novel. Murugan wants to disprove the theory that Ross discovered malarial parasites. Ultimately he comes to the conclusion that it is not Ross but Mangala, an assistant in Ross's laboratory who had used malarial parasites to cure Syphilis. She had done it with the help of a man called Latchman. So Mangala's secret investigation regarding the Syphilistic pattern, in Cunningham's laboratory and the observations how certain chromosomes were found in the non-generating tissue, the brain and could be transmitted through malaria are as Murugan calls them "The Calcutta Chromosome."

In the course of the novel Murugan explains to Urmila that Mangala stumbled on something that neither she nor Ronnie Ross nor any scientist of that time would have had a name for. It could be called a chromosome by analogy but Calcutta chromosome cannot be found by normal methods as it is not present in every cell. It is too deeply encrypted and the techniques used in laboratories cannot isolate it. It is not transmitted from generation to generation by sexual reproduction. It develops out of a process of combination and not in particular to every individual. So that only Murugan says that it could be found only by a person like Mangala. At the same time, as these biological correlates are not transmitted by sexual reproduction, it doesn't mean that they cannot be transferred between individuals by other methods. Mangala started at the deep end, by stumbling upon the process of transmission, rather than the chromosome, itself. She didn't know what a chromosome was, but it was malaria that led her to it. As the malarial bug has the capacity to cut and paste its DNA, it is very hard to develop to malarial vaccine. So that only Mangala began to use malarial parasite to cure syphilis. It is named Calcutta Chromosome by Murugan.

The novel's sub-title "A Novel of Fevers, Delirium, and Discovery" refers to the mystical aspect of the novel which presents a principle of science and counter-science. In the novel, Murugan says: "You know all about matter and anti-matter, right? And rooms and ante-rooms and Christ and anti-Christ and so on? Now let's say there was something like science and counter-science?"

In explicating his hypothesis of the 'Calcutta Chromosome,' a Chromosomal means of transmitting information, Murugan utters a Heisenberg-like uncertainty principle that seems to govern the writing without clearly articulating any particular alternative to genetics, culture, colonialism, Nobel scientists, and their relationship to the disease that continues to kill two or three million people every year.

Likewise, the fever, delirium and discovery are added to historical facts about malaria and the scientist Ronald Ross and his findings on malarial fever. *The Calcutta Chromosome* takes up the issue of the malarial fever and colours it with mysticism and mystery and supernatural and superstition. With this Ghosh emphasizes secrecy, mystery and self-contradictory knowledge and confronts what he calls conventional science with the ingenious knowledge and method of counter science. By the very term 'Chromosome' Ghosh means, the search for the ultimate transcendence, of nature and of immortality. With this he explains the failure of the body and migration therefrom. That is what he calls Calcutta chromosome. In it, Ghosh has picked up the topical issue of the recurrence of the malarial fever, and in the feverish delusion he has presented a secondary world in space and time.

The fantastic world of the novel presents a process of various thematic and technical experimentations and innovations. In this novel, Ghosh practices structural 'synaesthesia.' The novel has primarily the theme of search for immortality. The team of search for immortality moves through a list of female characters Mangala. Mrs. Aratounian, Urmila, Tara and so on. Similarly the male characters, Antar, Murugan, and Laakhan or Lakshman desire to attain immortality by performing something to the satisfaction of their own. Antar decides to dig the grave of Murugan which has been mysteriously closed under suspicion. Murugan wants to unearth the findings of Ross, especially related to malarial disease and his relation with Mangala and so on. Laakhan also wants to expose his identity by killing Phulboni and tries to achieve immortality by killing the station master and thereby making Phulboni write Laakhan stories.

The story of the novel weaves around the past, present, and the future. When the novel begins, the theme of immortality and identity are given importance. Antar, an Egyptian computer programmer and system analyst in New York, decides to find the identity of an I.D. card holder, Murugan. Further, he discovers that Murugan has suddenly disappeared on 21 August 1995, better known as 'the world Mosquito Day,' from Calcutta.

Murugan is deeply interested in malarial research, particularly he wants to expose the stand of Ronald Ross in relation to the malarial research. Later with the search, he proves that even before Ross the lady Mangala had been using malarial infection to cure Syphilis with the help of an assistant called Luchman or Laakhan, Mangala and Luchman/Laakhan/laxman/Lachan/ Lokhon were carrying out the experiment through an indigenous method. Their efforts prove one of the strong thematic points of the novel that, "if matter and science" were the stronghold of the accidental world 'anti-matter' and 'counter science' were controlled by the 'oriental.' Further, Mangala and Lutchman also carry the theme of immortality. The spirits of Mangala and Laakhan are reincarnated in Mrs. Aratounian and Roman Halder respectively. Further, the strategic weapon 'discourse of silence' is also used by Ghosh in the case of Mangala who under the cult of secrecy controls Ross, Grigson, Cunningham, and all male investigators of malarial parasite. She uses the potent weapon of silence to conquer all who come in her way. She in fact tries to find a cure for Syphilis parasite through counter science or faith. In her attempt, the novel highlights the theme of the rustic infiltration into the world of Science/knowledge to control the ultimate transcendence of nature, and proves the theory of 'migration of soul(s).' 'Transmigration of the soul is based on the assumption of transmigration of personality'—a chromosomal effect on the body and soul. This theme highlights the Indian theme of "Kalchakra' (the wheel of time) as Murugan and later Antar, the two computer experts, are chosen to be the subsequent Laakhans to the succeeding Mangala that is Urmila and Tara. In the whole novel, Ghosh employs 'Magic realism' to highlight the impossibility of the happening without losing the immediacy of its existence. In fact, Amitav Ghosh in *The Calcutta Chromosome* has rearranged the simplistic equation of life, death and immortality to prove that 'word manipulated' artistically can establish theories that are true and yet stranger than fiction.

Ghosh's novel also exemplifies the theme of science versus counter-science. In fact, Ghosh emphasizes secrecy, mystery, and self-contradictory knowledge and confronts what he calls conventional science with the ingenious knowledge and method of uneducated Indians. In the course of the novel Murugan's movements, ideas, beliefs, supposition, and inference reveal that it is not Ross but Mangala even before Ross who made researches on Malaria. The effort also involves "a high degree of fictional faking and the novelist tries to create a sense of spiritualism, belief in birth and rebirth and transposing and transcendence."

The novel is also based on the theme of disappearance and discovery. In fact, the whole novel is based on this theme in which Murugan, once disappeared on the World Mosquito Day, in 1995 discovers that it is not Ross who had discovered the malarial parasite but it is Mangala who had found it before Ross with the help of an assistant Lakhan. Even at the end, Ava shows Murugan, Urmila and Sonali rushing to the station Sealdah, where they are told Phulboni and Mrs. Aratounian have gone. This is the place from which Murugan has been recorded as missing, since August 1995 and is not heard of till his ID card appears on Ava's screen. Sealdah is the station from where Mangala and Laakhan were hired. It is the place which has caused most of the characters to disappear. What the novelist is talking about is a technology for interpersonal transference—the Calcutta chromosome.

Thus against all the incidents, experiments, and technical terms of the new technology, the novel presents these themes. The themes presented in the novel are the clues that are left to the imagination of the reader to find a probable solution.

Works Cited

Ghosh-Schellhorn, Marrina, 'Chromosome der Utopie: Utopische Entwurfe in der anglophonen Literatur Indien's in *Utopie und Dystopie in den neuen englischen Literature*, eds. Hans-Ulrich Seeber and Ralf Pordzik, Heidelberg: Carl Winter, 2002, pp. 275-87.

Ghosh, A. *The Calcutta Chromosome: A Novel of Fevers, Delirium and Discovery* (Delhi: Ravi Dayal, 1996; London: Picador, 1996).

'The Story Bug' (review of *The Calcutta Chromosome), New Statesman,* 6 September 1996, 47.

Clute, John, 'Excessive Candour: A Tale Decent Folk Can Buy' (Review of *The Calcutta Chromosome,* 1997).

Kich, Martin, 'Mosquito Bites and Computer Bytes: Amitav Ghosh's *The Calcutta Chromosome,' Notes on Contemporary Literature* (Carrollton, GA), 30, 4 (Sept 2000), 9-12.

Kumar, Gajendra, '*The Calcutta Chromosome.* A Strange Odyssey of Time and Mystery,' *Indian Writings in English, Vol. IX,* ed. Manmohan K. Bhatnagar and M. Rajeshwar, Delhi: Atlantic, 2000.

Lutwick, Larry I., Review of *The Calcutta Chromosome, Infections in Medicine,* 15, 3 (1998), 173.

Schumacher, Lyn, Review of *The Calcutta Chromosome, Foundation,* 71 (1997), 120-22.

Sen, Sudeep, '*The Calcutta Chromosome*,' *World Literature Today,* 71, 1 (1997), 221-22.

Chetan Bhagat: Society and Popular Culture

TAPAN GHOSH
University of Burdwan

"Whether you love him or hate him, chances are that you have read him," says Swati Daftuar in the front-page article on Chetan Bhagat entitled "The Revolution Man" (*The Hindu Magazine*, November 20, 2011). He might not be a literary purist, he has India sit up and notice him: "Bhagat has made India read." In an interview with Swati Daftuar, Bhagat shows a sense of pleasant surprise.

> He is taken aback by his popularity: I don't know what makes my books work. I enter a bookstore and I'm frankly overwhelmed by the number of books in most of them and I know people are buying mine. It's quite humbling. But if I had to guess, I'd say it's because I write about real people. The real middle-class India that has always been looking for a voice that is its very own.

Chetan Bhagat's novels are based on popular themes. Some of the themes are repetitive, like that of love but they are popular anyway. Each novel is basically a love story. Bhagat defends that: "youngsters treat their love-lives as one of their biggest priorities," which makes him choose love stories as the framework of his books.

The choice of the theme is the major reason of Bhagat's success. He writes about what he knows the best. In this respect, he reminds us of Jane Austen, who made her avowed aim to write about the life she knew the best. Her canvass is marriage and man-woman relationship in the 19th century England, which she was well-acquainted with, and in her fiction she never went beyond that. Bhagat too follows the same formula. For any author, says Bhagat, it is virtually impossible to write effectively about what he doesn't know: "I know middle-class Indian life first-hand. I know about the struggles of a student." Continuing, he tells Swati Daftuar:

> If you told me to write about Harry Potter, I couldn't. But then, J.K. Rowling couldn't write about IITs. I suppose the lucky bit here is that the India I know constitutes a large part of the country. My latest book [Revolution 2020] is about Varanasi, and that's a deliberate move on my part, because I noticed that while I have a large readership in towns, so far, I hadn't given them a voice in my books. I know most writers want to be published in the U.S. and U.K. after becoming famous in India, but for me, it's very important that even the smallest part of my own country experiences my own writings and feels like a part of it.

Bhagat weaves contemporary urban issues in each of his novels; the quality of private coaching centres, student suicides, misplaced ambition and rampant corruption. He also deals with urban cities and urban problems, inter-caste marriages, students hankering after professional jobs and making career choices. The younger generation, says Bhagat, is surrounded by the Internet, gadgets and video games. His raw material is more than that: "I try to incorporate a little of everything. A message, a story, humour—but make it so familiar that it's a pleasure to read at the same time."

While Bhagat is truly not a literary figure, he is well-acquainted with some classics. To a query as to who his favourite authors were, he says: "I like reading J.K. Rowling, Rohinton Mistry and Gulzar. I consider Gulzar as my role model. I am an avid reader of Joseph Keller's Catch 22 and might have read it more than 22 times. I have not read many classics." Bhagat's liking for Gulzar is perhaps out of his belief that a work of art should have an aesthetic appeal for a common man.

Bhagat's language is lucid and simple; he does not write in a complex or involved style. It is wrong to assume that a good writer has to write in an immaculate and near-perfect style. Unlike V.S. Naipaul, Salman Rushdie or Amitav Ghosh, he does not speak in coded metaphors and far-fetched allusions. In his writings, content is more important than the medium. Says Bhagat: "I don't use big complicated words. And that makes it easy to read them, even for people who aren't really readers."

While writing, Bhagat always keeps his readers in mind: who are the people reading Chetan Bhagat? In Bastar, Bhagat's books have been used to teach English to the tribal children. Bhagat is not pretentious about his mastery over the language as he thinks he writes in English because "yes, I'm most comfortable writing in English, but I'm equally comfortable with Hindi too. So it becomes possible for me to relate to a wider readership."

Chetan Bhagat is conscious that a vast majority of Indians is still illiterate and only a part of population knows English. After all, English is not our first language, and reading an English book is still a problem for most of the people. Says Bhagat: I write in simple, straightforward English, the kind that is easy for a beginner reader to understand. . . . I have never claimed to be the best writer there is. . . . I do write books that work because when a child wants to read a book about his country, a book that he can understand, a book that improves his English but doesn't overwhelm him, he picks up my books. I think that is important.

Chetan Bhagat is an avowed admirer of Yoga. Though quite busy with his writings, social life, and engagement with his wife and with his eight-year-old twins, he practises and advocates Yoga for all: "I do seek mental peace through reading. I, however, believe that students who are studying for I.I.T or other courses should do 'pranayam' and 'sadhana' (meditation) to keep themselves mentally fit. My novels have a lot of spiritual elements in them as I am a spiritual person."

Getting youngsters habituated to regular Yoga practice builds for them a lifetime of positive health and harmony. What's more, fitness becomes a way of life. They may be taught breathing exercises such as 'pranayam' and 'sadhana,' in addition to other Asanas. A positive physical health, says Bhagat, will improve academic performance of the students and pave way for their higher achievement in life.

Chetan Bhagat is quite popular with Twitter. He has as many as 1,762,382 followers. In the article "Limits of Freedom,' in India Today of 19 August 2013, Bhagat agrees that social media is playing a pivotal role in the country; but it is still a new platform and there are no rules of the game. Its offshoot therefore is a lot of abuse and personal attack on Twitter. This has often disrupted intellectual debates in social idea. While Bhagat stands by the right to freedom of expression, at the same time he seeks full protection, as a citizen, from the right to be protected from abuse.

Twitter has a great relevance and it is a substitute to the erstwhile 'coffee house culture.' In the eighteenth-century England, many writers like Dr. Johnson, Addison and Steele, used to interact with others and even write, sitting long hours in the coffee houses. It is true of the nineteenth-century France where French philosophers like Camus and Sartre as also American writers like Hemingway wrote their texts in the coffee houses.

One may argue, says Bhagat, that social media is an extension of a coffee house adda of the good old days. Twitter, he says, is even more powerful than just an adda. One comment by an author or politician can cause a reaction chain. It spreads like wild fire. For a common man, who had no say in yester-years, it is a great source of expressing his views. Bhagat refers to many youngsters who ask him if social media could lead to a revolution in India: "My answer is perhaps yes." Bhagat says that we "certainly need a revolution to rise above petty differences and prejudices."

While using the social media, one has to be very cautious as there can be reaction from your followers if you express your ideas or words in a 'loose' language. Recently Bhagat was criticized for using the word 'rape' to describe the rupee's free fall: "The rupee is asking, is there no punishment for my rapists?" Bhagat tweeted after rupee touched a new low, after inviting a barrage of angry reactions from many Twitter users who accused him of trivializing the gravity of rape crimes. They alleged that at a time when the Mumbai rape survivor was still recovering in hospital, using the 'rape joke' was improper and stupid. They felt that the word 'rape' should not be used so casually as Bhagat did. There were others who supported Bhagat and defended the rape metaphor in the context of poor state of economy. Earlier, Shobha De, the noted author, had used a similar terminology: "If the UPA government is forced to quit, does the Opposition possess a magic wand to fix the rupee-rape crisis."

Chetan Bhagat's novel *Two States* has a relevance for Mumbai film world. "The Mumbai film industry," says Sidharth Bhatia, "is often held up as a good exemplar of secularism and plurality. This is not a claim without merit." ("A Train of Thought," The Asian Age, 19 Aug. 2013) Bollywood accepts you without bothering about your caste, community, ethnicity or religion. It is a pity that there are not many films which tackle or even touch upon the subject. There are some exceptions, however. The latest one in this regard is Rohit Shetty's "Chennai Express," in which the boy is north Indian and the girl comes from a village in Tamil Nadu. The theme has really clicked and audience has welcomed it. No wonder, the film has collected more than 270 crores within first couple of weeks. Like the readers of *Two States*, the audiences have showered accolades on the story of the intercultural love affair. At a time when many groups and parties are promoting rifts between communities and trying to create a narrow definition of what constitutes a nation, a novel like *Two States* and a film like "Chennai Express" serve as a good antidote. These promote, without being preachy, the concept of multiculturalism and pluralism. Indians and those outside India have warmly endorsed the basic message of Bhagat's novel and Shetty's movie: cultural differences don't matter; we are basically one.

2 States has given a great impetus to the popular romantic novel. In the recent times, the readers have shown a great interest in romances, the desi love stories, written by Indian authors. A new crop of authors—Faraaz Kazi (Truly, Madly, Deeply), Anjali Kirpalani (Never Say Never), Anuja Chauhan (Those Pricey Thakur Girls)—have successfully handled the romance genre. Major reasons for the popularity of this kind of fiction are: changing values of the young generation, impact of the romantic films, comparatively a freer mixing up of the genders in the various walks of life and inter-caste marriages.

Chetan Bhagat has definite views on political affairs, like the reorganization of states in the country. The political manoeuvres have resulted into the division of Andhra Pradesh, India's fifth largest state both in area and population. Telangana became the 29th state in the Indian Republic in August 2013. Let us revisit Indian history during the mid-twentieth century. When a separate Andhra State was carved out of Madras Presidency in 1953 on linguistic basis, there was a demand for a separate Telangana State comprising the Telugu-speaking areas of Hyderabad State. It goes without saying that the decision to create a new state has been taken with an eye on political benefits. The bifurcation of the State is a farce. Why did it take the Congress so long to understand and fulfil the aspirations of the people of Telangana? It wanted to arrest its waning influence in Andhra Pradesh.

Chetan Bhagat finds it an undesirable step, for it is likely to have a deep and damaging impact on the national scene. The decision of the Congress-led government for the creation of a separate Telangana State will trigger a cascading effect with Statehood demands being roused across the country. It is giving rise to the breaking up of large states like U.P., M.P., Bengal, Maharashtra and Karnataka.

In the present-day competitive politics, it has become common for political parties to see their vote bank interests rather than public interests. Telangana creation will raise several demands: Bodoland in Assam, Vidarbha in Maharashtra, Mithilanchal in Bihar, Koorg in Karnataka, so on and so forth. India is so to say one, but with million mutinies. To claim that India has made an all-round progress is travesty of facts. We need to pay attention to serious issues; hunger, malnutrition, corruption, law and order. The world's most diverse and heterogeneous conglomeration of peoples can survive only if there is unity and respect for others. The turmoil over the formation of Telangana out of Andhra Pradesh is likely to shake the very foundations of an already unequal country.

Commenting on the bifurcation of the state, Bhagat in his article "The Telangana Effect: What India needs is not many new states, but a new state of mind" (The Times of India, 10 August 2013) makes a generalization, to begin with:

> An endearing, almost cute trait of Indians is that we never really lose hope. We always feel a messiah, or a great grand scheme will soon come and deliver us from our woes. It is a narrative reinforced by Bollywood, where somehow a hero works things out in the end. Our mythology too talks about good forces (God) with amazing powers coming and killing the evil (demons).

Bhagat wonders at the gullibility of people who feel convinced that the creation of a new state will offer solution to longstanding problems of the people in that region. Will such a step really do good to the miserable common man's life? It is the common man who is really suffering in India, and it is not easy to redeem his sufferings. In an exasperated move, some people like to believe that a "new state" might be handy to take care of various shortcomings. People fail to elect "good leaders" and do not find new criteria for governance over caste and regional prejudices.

With tongue-in-cheek, Bhagat says that "we will change none of this but somehow come to believe that solution to all our problems lies with one magic solution—a new state. With a firm conviction, he states: "What we have started now with Telangana is something so harmful, vile and terrible, we will all regret in the times to come if we don't check it now. And Bhagat is strongly against submission to threats and arm-twisting by a set of people: "What is a problem is coercive demands for a state, where sections of the population take on shrill voices, threaten violence or resort to strikes and try to gouge out a state for themselves. What makes it worse are a weak Centre and a PM who says or does little to quench such voices."

Bhagat likes to believe that while we may curb and control such movements, we should not be stemming them with undue authority and force. It is important to understand where such demands originate and if something can be done to address the underlying issues without constantly redrawing the map of the country.

So, why the sudden desire for so many states?, questions Bhagat. Well, the demand seems to be coming from economically backward pockets of the country People from that region might be so frustrated that they seek remedy in the formation of a new state. Perhaps it may alleviate their long-standing sufferings. Also they feel that a leader from their own kind may empathize with them and find an easier solution to their demands.

Bhagat begs to differ from this viewpoint. In his opinion, it is a "highly flawed thinking." We face all these problems only because we have not been fair or impartial in the selection of our leaders. At the time of elections, we do not search our conscience. We are swayed by caste, creed and community. We overlook the ability and qualities of the candidates. Rather, we vote one with whom we can identify ourselves in terms of community or religion. We never blame ourselves. It is always an external demon, and usually from the other community or caste that causes our woes and problems. Not us.

Bhagat feels hurt by the wilful split of Andhra Pradesh. Says he: "AP was a wonderful state by itself. Sure, it may have issues like any other state. Cutting it up, making many parts of India . . . hardly seems a solution." He admits that he is not totally averse to the creation of new states, but there should be a genuine reason to do so. Clinching the matter, Bhagat states in unequivocal terms: "the answer to India's problems is not a new state. It may be rather a new state of mind. A modern, unprejudiced, thinking Indian mind. Can we add that to the list of new state demands please?" Like poverty, new state is also a state of mind. It has psychological dimension and its solution lies elsewhere. No wonder, even our age is just a state of mind. This generation's greatest sartorial dilemma is the 'advancing age.' The concept has changed in the present times. Today, age has a different relevance—30s are the new 20s and 40s are the new 30s. Both men and women are looking younger and robust than in our parents' times. It is more important to dress and behave in a certain style that determines the state of mind.

In several ways, Chetan Bhagat is an epitome of India. He is popular with the Indian diaspora. Many NRIs when they periodically visit their native country carry back with them pickles and the books of Chetan Bhagat. Even the second and third generation of Indian diaspora, who have not visited India, get to know of India—its politics, religion and culture—through the writings of Chetan Bhagat. The popularity of Chetan Bhagat has given a great fillip to the growth of popular fiction and many publishing houses have launched novels in this category. Penguin Books, the best-known and a highly reputed company which caters to the audience, has brought out a wide variety of popular fiction under their new commercial imprint Metro Reads. These novels, being close to life and people, are quite relatable. Also, they have published romances, similar in vein, like Love over Coffee, No Deadline for Love, Losing Virginity and Other Dumb Ideas. Likewise, HarperCollins has brought out a number of 'easy reads,' like the novels of Anuja Chauhan. Her novels, like Bhagat's, are bestsellers and also being made into Bollywood films.

Anuja Chauhan (b. 1970), like Chetan Bhagat and Amish Tripathi, was a professional. She worked for seventeen years in media and advertising and is now a full-time creative writer. She launched her first novel *The Zoya Factor*, in the year 2008. She was born in Rajput family and like Bhagat studied in Army Public School. Her books are romances and portray glamorous elite world. She is labelled as a chic-lit writer, as her novels have a great appeal to the young generation, especially women in their 20s and 30s.

The Zoya Factor takes us to the world of advertising and cricket. It is the story of a bubbly girl working in an advertising agency who meets Indian cricket team through her job. It tells us about how love happens between a journalist and a member of the national cricket team.

Her second novel *Battle for Bittora* takes us to the nitty-gritty of Indian politics. It is a story of 25-year old Jinni who lives in Mumbai and works in an animation studio. Circumstantially and at the behest of her grandmother, she joins politics and falls in love with her adversary. It is an absorbing tale of young India, robust and hilarious.

Chauhan's latest novel *Those Pricey Thakur Girls* has again hit the jackpot. It has been in the list of bestsellers for last several weeks. It tells the story of Justice Laxmi Narain Thakur and his wife Mamta who spend their days watching anxiously over their five beautiful daughters named alphabetically, and of different temperaments but romantic at heart. They flit in and out of their spacious bungalow at New Delhi's prestigious Hailey Road. The story revolves around the fourth daughter Debjani, a newsreader at Desh Darpan (DD). The book brings about a lot of memories: our first TV, the Chitrahar days and the weekly movie on Sundays, when the whole family would be huddled in front of the TV. The novel is extremely captivating, with lot of wit and humour. Chauhan's characters are vibrant, colourful and hilarious. They have drawn immediate attention of the young generation.

Chetan Bhagat and Amish Tripathi are India's largest-selling authors. The two writers have some similarities. Amish Tripathi, better known for his Shiva trilogy—*The Immortals of Meluha*, *The Secret of Nagas* and *The Oath of the Vayuputras*—has emerged as 'another Chetan Bhagat.' His novels have sold more than 17 lakh copies. More recently, he made headlines for bagging Rupees 5 crore as advance for his next series of books from Westland. Like Chetan Bhagat, Tripathi is a banker-turned fulltime author, a household name. He too, like Bhagat, started writing along with his job as a banker. After his second book in fact, Tripathi earned more from royalty than the salary he was getting then, and he therefore decided to pursue writing as his career. While Bhagat takes common young man as his raw material, Tripathi's writings are derived from Hindu mythology.

While Chetan Bhagat is an alumnus of IIM, Ahmedabad, Amish Tripathi is from IIM, Kolkata. The management background has been immensely helpful to both the writers. In Indian market, where sale of books is limited, the sales of novels of both these writers have been enormous. Their marketing skills and self-projection have been widely credited for the success of their novels. Weeks before the release of his first novel, Tripathi printed sample copies of the first chapter and made it available free of cost to all those who were interested to have a look at it. It was something unprecedented, and the readers felt they had been taken into confidence about the contents and quality. In the case of Chetan Bhagat, the clientele has been mainly the young generation. Students and all those working in MNCs have found

Bhagat as their favourite author. Bhagat addresses contemporary issues which have great relevance to the younger lot.

Again, like Chetan Bhagat's novels, Tripathi's books are being adapted into films. The book The Immortals of Meluha is being made into a film by Dharma Productions. Tripathi is involved in writing of the film script too. In 2013, a music album called "Vayuputras," based on The Oath of Vayuputras, was released. The album has songs by noted singers like Sonu Nigam, Palash Sen and others. This was innovative: it was the first time ever that an original soundtrack had been made for a book series. The launch of Bhagat's novels is no less glamorous. There is wide publicity on hoardings, newspapers and grand book launches.

Is there a method in his writing? That is the most important question which strikes a common reader of Chetan Bhagat. Why does he have such a large readership? Many critics opine that the tribe of Bhagat and the likes do not have any literary merit. They are projected as easy reads, more of pastime stuff. That explains the success of publishers like Rupa, Srishti and India Log. They are meeting the demands of the public. But it is not to say that it is only commercialization of the project. "We can see more clearly," says Aditya Sudarshan (*The Hindu*, July 4, 2010), "that the push towards the new breed of writing is not being fuelled by market forces—those simply aren't strong enough." The impetus for new books, in his opinion, "comes from the readers, not from the writers." They serve a definite purpose.

It is evident that publishing of Indian novels has grown manifold. Many more new authors are being published than ever before, and in various genres. We have love stories, crime fiction, thrillers, young adult fiction, fantasies, erotica, chick-lit and graphic fiction. All this is significant fiction, notwithstanding light and less complicated. Of course, it is not serious—does not follow 'great tradition'—but good enough to bridge the 'divide' between literary and commercial fiction.

Films have traditionally invited comparison with other mediums of narrative expression. No wonder, a number of films have been based on popular novels. This has enhanced the value and popularity of both the novels as also the films based on these. Sri Lankan novelist Michael Ondaatje's novel *The English Patient*, Sarat Chandra's *Devdas*, Bankim Chandra's *Anandmath* and R.K. Narayan's *Guide* are best examples of this type. This tradition is best exemplified in the case of Chetan Bhagat. He is perhaps the only novelist whose all novels have been picked up by film companies to adapt them into films.

Bhagat's novel *One Night @ the Call Centre*, which received Young Achiever's award in 2004, was made into a film entitled "Hello," in the year 2008. This was followed by "3 Idiots" (2009), based on his novel Five Point Someone with Aamir Khan as hero. The film was a great commercial success, having set an all-time record by earning 385 crore rupees. The third novel The Three Mistakes of My Life was recently released as "Kai Po Che," which has been well received by the audience. His novel 2 States: The Story of My Marriage will be made into a film, to be released in 2014, with the cast of Arjun Kapoor and Alia Bhat.

The film "3 Idiots" has been so successful in the foreign market that it has sparked a global hunger for Indian films. It has turned to be a major hit in Japan. Released in May 2013 by Japan's oldest distribution company, Nikkatsu, it has grossed $ 1 million (Rs. 6.5 Crores) and is still being screened in that country. Inspired by the success of this film, many film distributors from Japan, Taiwan, Brazil, Hong Kong, Sweden, France, Germany, China and Korea are queuing up in big numbers at the Mumbai film mart. All these countries have joined the race to exhibit Indian films in their countries. It goes to the credit of Chetan Bhagat to have written a novel that has spurred interest among people not only in India but all over the globe.

Not only that, "3 Idiots" has now earned a new badge of honour as diplomatic courier between India and China. On 17 September 2013, External Affairs minister Salman Khurshid gifted visiting Chinese information minister Cai Mingzhao a copy of the Aamir Khan-starrer that underpins Prime Minister Manmohan Singh's persistent message to India's eastern neighbour—that there is enough geopolitical space for both nations to grow: "It's the perfect film for us to gift—both as a sign of our friendship, and in terms of the message it conveys."

The film that was Bollywood's most financially successful film till Shah Rukh Khan's "Chennai Express" steamed past it this year, is themed on the ceaseless competition in India's top higher education institutions. Students of a college in the film are repeatedly bombarded with the message that they must compete hard and view batch-mates as rivals to be beaten. Healthy competition is the core of success in our life. "Life is a race," the principal of the college famously says, "If you don't run fast, you'll get trampled." But the lead character, a student played by Aamir, instead encourages his friends to pursue their interests, and help each other. Chetan Bhagat has indeed been instrumental in nurturing DVD diplomacy with China.

In India, everyone pretends not to work hard, for hard work is not reimbursed. Getting good results by studying less implies that you are brighter than others. It is the end that is important than the means. Shortcuts or mugging up is more common than the actual process of learning in the class and absorbing lectures. This is the work culture, overall. You may not be doing your duty in the office, but keep up appearances that you are fully engaged. The fundamental mindset of an average Indian is that of a 'go-getter' and he has to be 'jugadu,' to bend the rules and circumvent them.

Chetan Bhagat draws our attention to the menace of corruption in our day-to-day life. In an article "Revenge of the Oppressed," published in The Times of India, dated May 18, 2013, he writes: "Why isn't corruption going away? The question baffles the educated middle classes. Why is a reasonable, Universal and noble demand for an honest society so different to achieve in a democracy?"

Sure, at one level everybody wants to remove corruption. Every Indian would like a clean society. However, says Bhagat, not every Indian feels it is the number one priority. It is the duty of the average man to elect honest leaders at the time of elections. Middle class feels concerned and makes efforts, to some extent, to bring in honest politicians. But a lot depends on the oppressed class which votes en masse for a candidate because he/ she belongs to their community or taken in by false promises or even instant gratification at the time of the elections: "many lower caste voters feel happy to see their community's candidate in power, as it makes life seem a little fairer after generations of oppression." The oppressed do want to remove corruption, but they want certain injustices fixed and other scores settled.

Bhagat feels sore that the present generation of youth, who want a corruption-free India, are denied opportunities as future has not much to offer to them. Will the situation ever change? Bhagat questions, but hastily adds: "Well, yes." We have, he feels, misdirected priorities. We need to make an all-out effort to remove corruption and people, from all communities and classes, have to forge a common front, rising above petty issues and controversies. Bhagat uses an apt analogy: "We do become one during cricket matches, and we have won the World Cup. If we can become one on this issue of fighting corruption, we will be able to win against it as well."

The reason behind the success of Bhagat's novels as also the films based on his novels is that he has a great appeal for a common man. "I think," says Bhagat, "I am the author of the masses. A person living in Karnal or Bhopal is reading my book. So, I also have to incorporate his/ her lifestyle in my writing." (*The Pioneer*, Feb. 11, 2008). He believes that the interest in Indian fiction is slowly picking up among the readers. Says he: "The kind of books I write are actually Indian literature. They are about the lives of people living here and not abroad. They are not tourist novels which are good but do not have a shelf life."

Cultural Confluence in Chetan Bhagat's *2 States: The Story of My Marriage*

SAKUNTHALA A.I.
M.P.M.M.S.N. Trusts College, Palakkad

Recent years have seen a proliferation of popular Indian English novels, depicting the many hazardous problems generated due to the difference of cultural aspects. Many of the Indian English writers of the present day have probed into the issues of cultural variation, and have portrayed how this variation affects humanity. Apart from this, they have also confirmed, through their novels, that the liberal values of 'Culture of Convenience' can solve the problems of cultural divergence, and that global harmony can be achieved by transcending the narrow borders of language and culture. Earlier novels witnessed a quest for identity regarding language, geography, community and culture. But the new generation writers want to break through all boundaries to create a global and universal culture.

Chetan Bhagat stands at the threshold of the confluence of two distinctly different cultures. While confronting the dissimilarities of North-South traditions, he also tells the readers of the cultural richness and variety of India. Like the postmodern interrogation of established conventions, he too questions the exclusivity of regions, language, food, dress, religious rituals and the rest of the community-specific codes that create insurmountable barriers in interpersonal relationship. In style too, he has opted for the everyday speech patterns of the present-day people who use Hinglish. Between literary aestheticism with classical precision and the practical approach of reaching one and all with simple diction, easy style and pragmatic themes, he has preferred to be an assertive individual with an intense desire to relate to his readers to build an emotional rapport. He writes with a purpose and is determined to address one and all with his easy style, simple language and the current issues which are to be solved both by parents and the youngsters. He is truly at the confluence of two states, cultures, approach to fiction writing and the use of Hinglish.

Chetan Bhagat has by now acquired almost a cult status with the young Indian readers. This 'biggest selling English language novelist in India's history,' as *New York Times* stated, has a meteoric rise from an investment banker to the most successful and popular writer in India within a short span of time. The reason for this phenomenal success is that he is an author who has touched a nerve with the young, ambitious middle class Indians. He is a writer who can sense the pulse of the youth and there is a lot of empathy a reader can feel with his real life-like characters. Bhagat has single-handedly changed the face of Indian fiction in the last few years with five best-selling novels to his credit, *Five Point Someone* (2004), *One Night @ Call Centre* (2005), *The 3 Mistakes of My Life* (2008), *2 States: The Story of My Marriage* (2009) and *Revolution 2020* (2011).

A writer who is seen more as a youth icon than just an author, Bhagat writes about India and for the Indians. He does not betray any serious literary ambitions. His novels, set in India's premier educational institutions, call centres or banks, address the everyday concerns of the youth, their choices and frustrations, moral, social and intellectual dilemmas. Many of these revolve around the lives of the educated, urban, English-speaking elite class. Characters are middle-class, usually young and grapple with some kind of identity crisis brought about by the "clash" of tradition and contemporary life.

Written in a language which is simple and lucid with tongue-in-cheek humour, Bhagat's fiction cannot boast of elite idiom of the intellectual litterateurs like Vikram Seth, Amitav Ghosh or Salman Rushdie. Bhagat's style may fall short according to the parameters of the legitimate literary standards, but his informal English has appealed to a wide spectrum of readers as it appeals more to the emotional make up rather than to the intellectual make up. He has definitely induced a reading culture among the young Indian reading public and his writings are drawn more of national readership than international acclaim.

Chetan Bhagat's fourth novel *2 States: The Story of My Marriage* relates to his life, where two youngsters belonging to different states of India fall in love, but the circumstances and family bondage make them not to take steps for inter-caste marriage. It is a typical Indian love story of a Punjabi boy, Krish Malhotra from Delhi and a Tamil Brahmin girl Ananya Swaminathan from Chennai, set against the backdrop of IIM. The novel tells us their struggle to marry over the jarring cultural and religious differences. They meet at the IIM cafeteria. Love blossoms and the duo decide to get married once they pass out of the college. But since they belong to 2 different states of India, the course of true love does not run smooth.

In India, a marriage is not between a boy and a girl, but between two different communities. Even though caste system has been legally abolished in India for more than 60 years, caste is cast in stone. Inter-caste marriages are still considered taboo for the orthodox Indian mindset.

Contrary to the usual practice, the two lovers do not elope, instead choose to seek the consent of their families. The hazards seem unfathomable in the beginning, because of the problems posed by cultural, religious and regional divide. A wedding in India is a complex affair that involves more than just the bride and the groom—it includes every member of both families. Bhagat writes: "Love marriages around the world are simple.

Boy loves girl, girl loves boy. They get married. But in India, there are a few more steps: Boy loves girl, girl loves boy. The girl's family has to love the boy. The boy's family has to love the girl. The girl's family has to love boy's family. The boy's family has to love girl's family. Girl and boy still love each other. Then they get married."

For this Krish has to figure out a way to fit into a traditional south Indian family and Ananya must try to compete with her Punjabi counterparts. Krish has a tough time convincing his mother who is prejudiced against dark-skinned Madrasi girls and wants her son to marry one of the wealthy fair-as-milk Punjabi girls. At the same time Ananya's parents wish their daughter married off to a well-settled Tamil boy. After a few desperate attempts in the beginning, finally he succeeds in his mission by taking tuitions for Ananya's brother, by helping her father to prepare a Power Point Presentation for his office and finally giving her mother a chance to sing in a concert organized by his office. In the meantime, Ananya also succeeds in winning the hearts of Krish's family members by helping one of his cousins to get married.

Now as they have convinced both their parents, they plan a get-together to Goa, but there also some verbal explosions take place between the two mothers and again the prospect of their marriage is jeopardized. The final breakthrough is when Krish's father comes to his rescue by giving him a pleasant surprise. Finally the two families are convinced and the nuptial knot is tied with the blessings of both parents. When Ananya gives birth to twin children, the hospital authorities ask them to which state they belong. For this Krish's reply is that the children belong neither to Delhi nor to Chennai, but to a much bigger state—India, implying that Indianness surpasses all the divisions of states.

Marriages are regarded as the most important social custom and hence viewed as the best means to remove the barriers of caste system. Love knows no boundaries whether it be of caste, creed, religion or region. Successful marriage is not dependent on caste, creed, religion or region; on the other hand, it is built on the aspects of mutual understanding and compatibility.

Bhagat has touched some of the sensitive issues of cultural differences especially in the case of marriages. The story is partly autobiographical, but the theme is universal. Although times have changed a lot, thanks to the scientific and technological advancements, the attitude of the people is still rooted in the past. Unless and until these deeply embedded ideologies are erased, we cannot outgrow our old mindset. The author opines that India needs a cultural revolution to change the people's orthodox minds. Unlike a revolting revolutionary, he tries to intermingle practicality, humour and genuine love. For the union of two families he chooses the mild but strong path of assimilation. Bhagat is not protesting against the old traditional culture, but he is trying to bridge the gap between the past and the present for a better future. Homogeneity is vital in a country's onward progress and this novel *2 States: The Story of My Marriage* is a social comment on homogeneity.